Unbolting the Dark, A Memoir

On Turning Inward in Search of God

Lynne Spellman

HAMILTON BOOKS

A division of
THE ROWMAN & LITTLEFIELD PUBLISHING GROUP
Lanham • Boulder • New York • Toronto • Plymouth, UK

Copyright © 2011 by
Hamilton Books
4501 Forbes Boulevard
Suite 200
Lanham, Maryland 20706
Hamilton Books Acquisitions Department (301) 459-3366

Estover Road
Plymouth PL6 7PY
United Kingdom

All rights reserved
Printed in the United States of America
British Library Cataloging in Publication Information Available

Library of Congress Control Number: 2011928605
ISBN: 978-0-7618-5584-2 (paperback : alk. paper)
eISBN: 978-0-7618-5585-9

∞™ The paper used in this publication meets the minimum
requirements of American National Standard for Information
Sciences—Permanence of Paper for Printed Library Materials,
ANSI/NISO Z39.48-1992.

In memory of Marjorie, my mother
1922-1960

Contents

Acknowledgments	vii
Chapter 1	1
Chapter 2	7
Chapter 3	12
Chapter 4	16
Chapter 5	20
Chapter 6	24
Chapter 7	28
Chapter 8	32
Chapter 9	36
Chapter 10	40
Chapter 11	45
Chapter 12	49
Chapter 13	54
Chapter 14	58
Chapter 15	62
Chapter 16	66

Chapter 17	70
Chapter 18	74
Chapter 19	78
Chapter 20	83
Chapter 21	87
Chapter 22	91
Chapter 23	95

Acknowledgments

Near the beginning of this project, poet Rebecca Newth suffered through several drafts as she taught me how to transform my scholarly prose into narrative. As the manuscript approached completion, philosopher Martha Nussbaum offered great encouragement and sage advice about finding a publisher. Along the way, the manuscript was also read, in whole or in part, by numerous other friends and colleagues, including Irene Fleming, Cintra Pemberton, Suzanne Stoner, Elizabeth Payne, Lynne Rudder Baker, Lynn Huber, Elliott West, Barbara Lewis, Pat Wyatt, Gail Tolleson, Jennifer Tolleson, David Chappell, Kaye Bernard, Lorrie Slaymaker, and Ed Minar. Joshua Daniel and Jenna Daniel helped me with proofreading, and Hope Christiansen of the World Languages, Literatures, and Cultures Department checked my French. I am grateful to all of them. I also want to thank Tom Breidenthal and Mitties DeChamplain for inviting me to present chapter one to their class on spiritual autobiography at General Seminary more than a decade ago and to the members of the class for their most helpful comments.

The University of Arkansas provided research support through two academic years, 1992-93 and 2001-02, and also granted the leave of absence which allowed me to attend seminary in 1997 and 1998. While at seminary I did work on Gregory of Nyssa which was published in *The Journal of Neoplatonic Studies* in 2000-03. Stripped of argument, scholarship, and connection to a wider set of issues, the understanding of what it might mean to progress infinitely toward God and to see God in the mirror of the self which are presented here were worked out in that paper. I remain grateful to the late Richard Norris, for sharing some of his vast knowledge of patristics with me while I was at seminary. Finally, I want to thank my editors at Hamilton and their colleagues for believing in the manuscript and for their expertise.

Time has brought changes. No one now could wander alone around Stonehenge as I did twenty years ago. Osage Forest of Peace is no longer a community of Benedictine nuns. But these things were then as I portray them. At midlife I was keeping a journal, and those journals were the starting point for this memoir. Though memory can distort events, a commitment to fidelity seems to me essential to the genre of memoir, and I have tried to keep that commitment.

I want to thank those who have allowed their names and their stories to be used, where their stories intersect with mine. In this regard, I am especially grateful to Jim, as the years I describe were a difficult time in our lives. Because I have changed no names, I have asked permission in every case where there seemed reason to do so, starting with Sr. Maatje who, on behalf of the community at Grandchamp, read a draft of what would become several chapters in this narrative while I was living there in 1992-93. I should add that I have made an effort not to misquote anyone (which is one reason there is so little direct quotation) or to intrude into others' lives more than was necessary.

The title is derived from Dylan Thomas's line "And love unbolts the dark," which is found in "Poem on his birthday." My awareness of the poem I owe to Jim.

Chapter 1

"You won't be going to school today." St. Augustine would have described these words as inwardly present in the storehouse of my mind. But I do not find in my memory the rest of that conversation, the part that mattered. Was it just before, or afterward? I do not know. My father told me that my mother had died.

I have done with my life mostly what I thought I wanted to do. I fell in love, and Jim and I married. I went through graduate school in philosophy and became a philosophy professor. Yet at thirty-eight, my mother's age when she died, I was overtaken by an unwelcome, disruptive restlessness. Even as I found myself wondering if my life had any meaning, I was filled with inchoate longing.

Although I had taught the arguments for and against the existence of God dozens of times, the question whether there is a God began to take on urgency for me. I asked myself whether Plato's claims about the Good, the summit of his unseen Reality, might be true. Looking back twenty years later, it is easy to see that my longing for the transcendent and for my mother are inextricably linked. I have learned how in late antiquity, for both pagans and Christians, knowing oneself by "turning inward" was considered a way of knowing God. At thirty-eight, I would have said, "If my yearning is for my mother, it cannot be for God." I no longer think that this is so.

That fall I had just returned from the previous year's sabbatical, although, actually, I never left town. But I stayed away from the campus, and I had long been in the habit of staying away from church. I knew from the parish newsletter that the Episcopal campus chapel had a new priest named Bill, who practiced a form of contemplative prayer. Bill taught that mental repetition of a phrase would make prayer wordless and as continuous as breath itself. The newsletter left me curious, and anxious, even repelled. My only knowledge of contemplative prayer had come from *Franny and Zooey*. I was surprised to learn that *The Way of the Pilgrim*, the book that captivated Franny, and the Jesus Prayer, whose effects it describes, exist.

Bill was attentive and still throughout the conversation that soon followed. Never have I met anyone who could be so still. I asked him, "Why should I think there is a God?" "I will not argue with a philosopher," he replied. Then he added, "But I can teach you to pray."

Is there a God to whom to pray? Again and again from junior high through graduate school, I had asked that question. In freshman music history I encountered the mass in the purity of Renaissance polyphony that images eternity in the world of time, making the beauty of God audible. I was drawn to an Episcopal Church by the Eucharist and a choir that could sing Palestrina. I appreciated the openness about theology I found there. As I was starting graduate school, I decided to join the Episcopal Church. The day before confirmation, I confessed to the priest that I did not believe. "Are you certain there is no God?" he asked. "No," I replied. "Then come and see," he told me.

I am sure old Fr. Arvedson expected I would see. But in the early 1970's, philosophy seemed in conflict with religion. I came to know too well that the proofs of the theist were, at best, problematic. Logical positivism was still influential; to be meaningful, an assertion was said to need empirical evidence, but "there is a God" cannot be tested.

After graduate school, I became part of the philosophy department at the University of Arkansas where teaching and publication claimed all my time. When a new dean wanted to emphasize research, although I was only three years out of school, I was appointed to be the department chair. Still, in all my preoccupation there remained a half-acknowledged strand of yearning. Though I no longer went to church on Sundays, or Christmas, or Easter or in Lent, as the seasons slid toward winter, I would wander in for days whose names evoked the mystery of transcendence: St. Michael and All Angels, All Saints, the Epiphany. Caught between wonder and embarrassment, as I watched, I pretended a sort of casualness. Now Bill too was saying: Come, and see.

I admitted to Bill that, in college, when I read *Franny and Zooey*, I had actually tried the Jesus Prayer, to no effect. Later I read somewhere that meditation would bring about the "relaxation response." But prayer without ceasing? At midlife the idea seemed to me both reckless and absurd. Yet if I walked away, could I be certain, entirely certain, that Bill had nothing to teach me?

Sometimes there are choices that are unrepeatable and important and worthy of risk. William James argued that religious belief might be like that.

In Bill I had happened to meet someone who knew about praying without ceasing, and it seemed unlikely to happen again. "[For propositions that cannot be decided on intellectual grounds, to say], 'Do not decide, but leave the question open,' is itself a passional decision—just like deciding yes or no,—and is attended with the same risk of losing the truth," wrote James. To experience the presence of God, if there were a God, seemed the very sort of thing James called a "momentous option."

When I was young, I liked to visit my parents' friend Irolene MacKenzie. Her apartment was full of wondrous mementos. Widowed and wealthy, she had traveled to Nationalist China, Thailand, India, Egypt, Australia, Brazil. In the late 1950's she declared herself ready to go to the moon: "They only have to get me there—I do not care if I come back." I do not have Irolene's spirit. I always want to go knowing I can come back, but I did not get my way. The more I meditated, the more I experienced being still, and the more stillness I experienced, the more I needed to meditate. The act of breathing was, as Bill had promised, becoming prayer. Yet month after month I continued to ask, "Why should I think there is a God?"

On campus at St. Martin's Episcopal Chapel, students gathered to meditate. It was never a large group, and one morning only Bill and I were there. When we had finished, I said, "I can hardly believe I am saying this, but I have come to realize there's a God." I said it not quite knowing what to say. I knew that to say it so untethered my past beliefs that I could scarcely think, but I did it because of something that had happened. The night before I had been alone in our basement garage. I was lifting weights, not the most likely time for an experience of God, but working out was when I had solitude. I was feeling very alone when suddenly it seemed to me that, beyond my seeing, something Holy was present. That night I found myself unexpectedly, inexplicably, in the presence of love, intense love, and I was sure that it was not my love.

I do not know whether I believed in God that morning at St. Martin's. I was so full of uncertainty. From the content of an experience, can one know if things are really as they seem? Most of my colleagues, indeed the majority of contemporary philosophers, do not find the claim of God's existence credible, and this caused me anguish. I considered contemporary philosophers to be the experts on the question, but that they would have been persuaded had they all had my experience I could not convince myself. Even the willingness to learn prayer had been worrying. I feared it a way of presupposing what was to be proved, of biasing evidence or judgment, a way that nurtured illusion.

Philosophers at the time tried to model philosophy on science, whose success we envy. Looking back, I still believe that philosophers should seek truth, and I think we sometimes find it. But as regards the existence of God and many other philosophical questions, I, like a lot of philosophers now, doubt that modeling philosophy on science can succeed.

Our sense of how things are, of what is plausible and what is not, may depend less on rational thought than I used to suppose. I have learned, for example, that my unfelt anger at events long past had influence I could not see. But the condition of the seeker is not the only consideration; there is also the nature of what is sought. What if a method for the search for truth subverts discovery of the most important truth? What if there is a God but knowledge of God's existence comes not by inference, but in relationship? What if knowledge that there is a God requires recognition? Might God be present but not intruding, waiting to be welcomed or ignored? These questions weighed on my mind. If it was God that I experienced, not to respond would be rejection, not just of a position, but of a person.

At the time I was thinking about these things, I knew almost nothing about mysticism. I had read William Blake in college, but his poetry I found obscure. And Wordsworth's "Tintern Abbey" had been almost as perplexing:

> And I have felt
> A presence that disturbs me with the joy
> Of elevated thoughts; a sense sublime
> Of something far more deeply interfused,
> Whose dwelling is the light of setting suns,
> And the round ocean and the living air,
> And the blue sky, and in the mind of man:
> A motion and a spirit, that impels
> All thinking things, all objects of all thought
> And rolls through all things.

What helped me to interpret my experience that night in our garage was instead a children's classic, *The Wind in the Willows*.

As Mole and Rat are searching for the lost baby otter, just before dawn, Ratty hears a strange celestial music that rouses in him a longing so full of pain and joy that nothing seems worthwhile except to listen to it forever. At first Mole says he hears only the wind playing in the reeds, but then he hears something else and he stops and bows his head.

If Mole had continued to insist that it was but the wind, would he have seen the Divine Presence, protecting the baby otter? Having lost my mother, did it unconsciously matter to me that something divine caught up Rat's "helpless soul and swung and dangled it, a powerless but happy infant in a strong sustaining grasp"? Later I would give thought to why in graduate school I had so internalized a methodology for knowing that fought with my own inner understanding. But before I could ask that question, I needed to learn to trust what I had rejected in myself.

Bill had read the desert fathers, but I was frightened by their ascetic excesses. I was appalled by St. Simeon Stylites, who sat for years atop a pole. Jungian psychology was important to Bill, yet Carl Jung's thought was so unlike anything I had studied that I could not make sense of it. But Bill's homilies were also filled with Zen stories, and a few of these I understood.

A master gives his disciple a gift, and because the room in which he places it no longer looks right, he changes the furnishings. Then the house needs to be remodeled to match the room, and the garden that surrounded the house redesigned, and the neighborhood transformed. Bill taught me contemplative prayer. He convinced me to go on retreat to Osage Monastery, a Benedictine community near Tulsa, and he was slowly persuading me that if I wanted to know God I needed to know myself. What were the implications for my life that Bill was giving me not one gift, but three?

Socrates believed that it is by knowing what virtue is that we become virtuous, and he thought of himself as a gadfly whose God-given task was to urge his fellow Athenians to care most of all about the state of their souls. When Socrates urged his listeners to know themselves, what he was asking them to do was to consider how to live.

Plato, Socrates' greatest follower, thought that knowledge of the Good is already within us; our task is to recollect. In late antiquity when both Stoic and Platonic patterns of thought were assimilated by Christian writers, the Socratic demand to know oneself took a personal turn, and St. Augustine's *Confessions*, written at the close of the fourth century, became the pattern for the literary genre of spiritual autobiography. In the same century, St. Gregory of Nyssa argued that the way we progress toward knowing God is by becoming pure in heart; God can be seen in the mirror of the self.

I continue to think about why in antiquity knowing oneself was held to be a way of coming to know God and what we mean if we make that claim now. I have come to question assumptions I used to have about "the self." Someday I would like to examine, with all the clarity philosophy can bring, the meanings that the church fathers gave to being "made in the image of God."

Some of my students would ask: "Why do you not concern yourself with all the world's great religions? You have limited yourself to the Christian spiritual tradition, but how, without examining all other religions, can you judge that Christianity is nearest to truth?" The answer is that I cannot. As it happens, I learned contemplative prayer from an Episcopal priest who had studied Zen. I have taught an honors course on Thomas Merton, who studied Buddhism and met the Dalai Lama. Nevertheless, my knowledge of the world's religions is at most superficial, and it would take longer than the remainder of my life for that to be remedied.

To know a religious tradition, any religious tradition, is not just to have a grasp of its concepts and doctrines. Understanding a religious tradition emerges from living it. To lay claim to Christianity can be to think about what needs to be discarded. It is also to look for what has been forgotten but is worthy of being retrieved. Gregory of Nyssa argued, to my mind persuasively, that we cannot know the essence of God. I think of Christianity as a gesture toward an Unfathomable Love that pulls on us.

Chapter 2

The sign read "Osage Monastery, Forest of Peace." I would not have found it had Bill not drawn a map. In childhood, the long black habits worn by the nuns at the neighborhood convent used to frighten me. Approaching Osage, I was anxious. I had been meditating for more than two years when Bill finally persuaded me to visit the monastery. The prioress, Sr. Pascaline, would direct my retreat. At our first meeting, she asked, "Are your parents living?" I said, "My mother died when I was twelve." Pascaline's next question was beyond all imagining: "Can you be grateful for your mother's death?"

My mother made my Raggedy Ann. She read to me books I still remember. She knew the name for every wildflower in the woods. From grade school I would run home to tell her all about my day, even the games we played at recess. I wish I could remember the sound of her voice and more of what she would say.

The summer before I began sixth grade, she had a mastectomy, and radiation treatment burned her skin. She assured me she would soon be well, but that did not happen. My first weeks of junior high, I walked from school to the hospital. Then I was told she was too sick to have me come. My father made long distance calls to my aunts and grandfather, all of whom hastily arrived in Omaha. They stayed at the hospital through the night. No one said that my mother was dying. In the morning I was told that she had died.

At Osage, Pascaline gave me a verse to ponder: "In the wilderness you saw Him, how Yahweh carried you as a parent carries a child all along the road you traveled on the way to this place." By day I walked in the woods and asked if that was true. At night I stared at the walls of my cabin; I hardly slept at all. To read the Bible did not comfort me. I found I could not pray. The place called Heaven to which she had gone seemed more remote than Australia or the moon. It seemed terribly far away. I knew that my mother did not want to die, but I did not comprehend how abandoned I still felt. Alone with myself at the monastery, I simply lay on the floor and cried.

The Catholic Benedictine community at Osage gathered for prayer in the morning, at noon, before supper, and at night. There were short services of Psalms and readings from Christian and Hindu scripture, along with hymns and prayers. "Who is this who sees behind the eyes, who hears behind the ears?" This antiphon, sung after the Psalms, is lodged forever in my mind. It is a question I cannot answer. Besides these services, traditionally called offices, there was a daily Eucharist. They also meditated together twice a day, each time for an hour, in silence. The morning meditation period began at 5:15 a.m., and although guests did not have to attend, I was always there. I had decided beforehand not to call Jim or anyone, and apart from the midday meal and supper, all week I was in silence. Time stretched in the emptiness, and my departure seemed far away. Then on the morning I was to leave for Arkansas, Pascaline, who had lived at an ashram in India, proposed that she anoint me.

I must have been anointed when I was confirmed in the Episcopal Church. But Pascaline did not just anoint my forehead, as would have been done then. She anointed all my senses, my heart, my hands, and my bare feet. When she had finished anointing my feet, she said, "This is for your mother." Then she bent down, and unselfconsciously, untheatrically, she kissed my feet.

Before I left, Pascaline warned me that my week had been so intense that upon my return to Fayetteville I might encounter trouble. When she said it, I could not think why that should be true. But within a week, Jim and I were in marital crisis, and on the campus I no longer felt at home. Within two weeks I was in therapy, and Jim and I sought marriage counseling. I could not return to what I knew, and I did not know what to do next. Jim, an only child, was depressed by his father's death and preoccupied with his mother's failing health. He wanted me to be as I had been. I could not explain to him the emotional turmoil I was feeling. Indeed, I did not understand it myself. Months passed while we made a pretense of being a couple. The college of arts and sciences at the university offered women faculty a fellowship to Cambridge, and I applied. Jim decided that the next academic year he would return to Illinois.

At the end of the following summer, I helped Jim move into a small apartment in Urbana-Champaign. Ever since Osage, I had longed to be in a monastery, and I arranged to visit several Episcopal religious communities before flying to London from New York. Jim took me to the train as I left for Chicago. Three weeks as a guest of various communities brought no clarity at all. Nonetheless, I called Jim from Cambridge to say I wanted to enter a religious community. I told him that I wanted to divorce.

That year I was a visiting fellow at Lucy Cavendish College, Cambridge, there to finish a book on Aristotle. Every day I walked awe-struck past the magnificent Gothic architecture of John's and Trinity and King's. I heard King's College choir not once, like a tourist, but day after day. I audited Myles Burnyeat's seminar on Plato's *Euthydemus* and eagerly attended a public lecture on cosmology by Stephen Hawking, which, like almost everyone else in the huge audience, I could not comprehend. Between the fall and winter terms, I traveled by train and ferry to the Isle of Skye, a treeless, misty, rocky, boggy plateau, and then through the mountains of the Lake District to the cliffs of Cornwall, where I hiked in wind and rain. With a Eurail pass, in the spring I went from Florence to the paradise which is Lugano, then north through Denmark. Before returning to England, I took a boat along the fiords of Norway.

Europe could have been idyllic, and at times it was. At Stonehenge I lingered until I was alone and took photographs at sunset. Those ancient stones were indecipherable remnants of a lost past, and they seemed expressive of the inaccessible past within myself. But instead of trying to become better established in my profession, as my university intended, all year I was haunted by a loss of meaning. I began by attending the evening seminar in the classics department for translation and discussion of Aristotle. I knew it would be good to try to make connections with other scholars and improve my facility with Greek. The topic that term was Aristotle's view of heat.

Aristotle's theory of heat affected his understanding of reproduction which influenced his metaphysics, and his metaphysics is foundational for much of Western thought. Nevertheless, whether Aristotle's theory of heat was worth thinking about was the only question the debate produced in me that year. I found the classics faculty at Cambridge to be welcoming and did not experience the disdain for American academics of which I had been warned. But when I was invited to give a paper to the centuries old B-Club, I knew it was an honor to be asked, and yet I did not respond. Although I was working steadily on Aristotle, I never even set foot in the world renowned Cambridge library. I wanted, most of all at Christmas, for Jim to call me, and I wanted him not to. I wanted, and did not want, to call him.

At Lucy Cavendish there were many formal dinners, whose purpose was primarily participation in intellectual conversation. Seating was sometimes assigned and sometimes changed after every course. At St. Bene't's where I worshipped, I met Br. Tom, a Franciscan, who recommended some Anglican women's communities; in the monasteries meals were eaten together in silence. I visited those places that no one finds unless one is seeking them. No one knew I was a philosopher and no one asked. Yet even though weekends in their guesthouses were sustaining me through the months at

Cambridge and I was drawn to their silence and prayer, the idea that the nuns never, or rarely, left the convent grounds felt confining and terrifying to me. I was uncomfortable with the vow of obedience, and I balked at the thought of wearing a habit instead of my jeans. I talked to novice mistresses and prioresses throughout England. All of them believed I had a vocation although they were not sure quite to what. When the abbess of the Benedictine community at West Malling asked me about my marriage, I told her how Jim once rescued an insect trapped in a latrine. She replied that she did not think that our marriage was over.

As I look back on the events of that year, it is almost as if they did not happen. I now find them hard to comprehend. Admittedly, Jim and I were failing one another, and I was lonely. Ten years as department chair had left me discouraged and exhausted, and I was finding philosophy arid. I never met my grandmothers nor do I have sisters, and having spent all my working life in a mostly male profession, in the religious communities I was enjoying just being around women. Besides all that, I was reading Thomas Merton.

I had not yet discovered Merton's disillusionment with monastic structure and his conflict with his abbot. I knew only the young Merton who idealized monastic life. Still, everyone assured me that to have a monastic vocation one must feel called to a particular community, and that never happened. Years later it is clear to me that I confused a vocation to live in community with a love of the shared silence that was turning perception inward. My longing for the monastery was pure yearning for the transcendent, which I projected on a way of life, aided by Merton's magnificent prose.

Monasticism was attraction to the holy as I had experienced it at Osage. It was a desire for union with God, and in my experiences of God, the memory of my mother is buried. In childhood I had locked the door to the room in which I stored a grief too great to grieve, and at midlife the part of myself which was left for me to live in had become unbearably small. I needed my life to be on hold for eight or nine years while I sorted things out, but in real life, searching out monastic communities all over England was part of the sorting. Monastic life became for me confused with love because Pascaline's actions had unconscious resonance which made the monastery "home."

I canvass these thoughts because my actions caused a lot of suffering. I am reluctant to absolve myself by declaring that both Jim and I needed our years apart (or worse, that it was somehow meant to be) even though we did both grow. I am reluctant to say that the pull of monasticism was really all about priesthood, although I do believe that I have been called to be a priest and staying at monasteries became part of my formation. I do not know what other roads were possible or where they would have taken me.

Chapter 2

All I know is the road that I followed, and I am grateful for where it has led. And of this I am certain: I could not have ignored my mother's death forever.

In winter between the terms at Cambridge, I rode across Rannock Moor in Scotland. From the window of an all but empty train, as I watched the mist which hid the distant mountains and clothed the rough brown grass, I sensed the closeness of Christ to me and all creation. I saw that everything is holy and to be treated with reverence. Returning by train from a weekend in Kent at the hermitages of the Sisters of the Love of God, I reached London's Charing Cross Station so disoriented by God's presence, a love which had physical weight, that I could not comprehend the flow of London traffic or understand the lecture on Aristotle I had returned to hear.

In June, the last ten days before I was to leave for the States, at the advice of a friend, I flew to Geneva to visit Grandchamp Monastery, a Protestant women's community in Switzerland. When the fall semester began at the University of Arkansas, I was often asked whether I was eager to return to Cambridge. To acknowledge the attractions of Cambridge was easy. Beyond that, I did not want to explain.

Chapter 3

Jim and I agreed that we would divorce as soon as I returned from England. I sought out a lawyer, but the interview left me distraught. "You should rush to be the first to file," the lawyer advised. "Tell Jim he will have to remove his woodworking tools from your garage." I was angry with Jim and he with me, but I knew he had no room for a table saw in his tiny apartment. Besides, we so trusted one another that in all the months we had been apart, we had never even separated our finances.

On Christmas Eve, the winter before I went to Cambridge, when we had eaten our traditional meal and unwrapped the gifts beneath the tree, too burdened to pretend, we talked of all that was troubling us. Jim wanted to have a child, something I had wanted some time before when he did not, but by that winter such a commitment sounded imprisoning. As I was almost forty-two, we could both sense that my answer would be irrevocable. For a while we sat together in our aloneness and sorrow that could not find resolution. What is left when words do not bring communion? Jim and I made love, communication which invokes no plans or points of view. When after seventeen Christmases together, the conversation failed, how else was there to say that, despite the separateness which was being wrought from our unity, there was another arithmetic, one where one divided by two was still one?

The semester that followed my return from Cambridge crawled to an end amid indecision. At Christmas I stayed at St. Margaret's on Cape Cod, and afterward I attended the American Philosophical Association meeting in New York. Jim was in Brooklyn, visiting his mother that same week. He telephoned me at the Marriott. We agreed to meet beneath the lions of the New York City Public Library on the last day of the year.

Chapter 3

Sitting on the library's steps, I watched him approach. We had not seen one another for sixteen months, but our clothes still looked alike—our parkas bought on sale from Pack Rat, his blue, mine brown, our North Face backpacks, the same but for size, our sweat socks, once shared. Together we crossed Fifth Avenue to a small cafe, nearly empty at midmorning.

"When you called from Cambridge and said you wanted a divorce, for a long time I supposed you did not mean it," Jim began. "As the months went by, I concluded that you did. Have you been happy this past year?" In our marriage I had always felt a child, and he, eight and a half years older and outwardly self-assured, seemed too much the parent. Finally, at forty-three I had been able to feel forty-three, and that, at least, was good. "But in England in the places you would have liked," I said, "I thought of you."

Jim was listening quietly, not interrupting me. Then he spoke of depression and abandonment. He told me what had made him angry, most of all. "Who else could know, who else would ever care, just what our dogs looked like or how much rust there was on that old VW?" My leaving, he said, had taken his past; I had taken away his past.

One summer we lived on a farm that belonged to my family. Jim taught me to drive our stick shift Beetle while we were there. The Christmas before we moved to Fayetteville in northwest Arkansas, we drove the VW from Illinois to the philosophy meetings in New York. In the mountains of Pennsylvania, Mopsy and Goliath romped in the falling snow as we pitched our tent by lantern light. Even had we found a place that would take dogs, we could not afford a room in a motel. In Arkansas we learned to sail, and Jim helped me prepare lectures on Aristotle. One year we reshingled the roof of our first house. It was a project that took all fall. In fact, we were on the roof pounding nails when the phone call came telling me I had been recommended for tenure.

I would rather be with Jim than anyone. He can take the ordinary moment and hear it sing. We were companions. Yet we did not know, how much we did not know, how to befriend one another against the ghosts that stalked us, harrying our years. In New York that day we talked perhaps an hour, little more. We agreed to meet again. Before we parted, he for JFK, I for Penn Station, we kissed. He pulled my ears, and I told him to take care of himself; he had a cold. When he was in New York to visit his mother, he always had a cold.

We met from time to time in the months that followed, converging at a Missouri park—like migratory birds, Jim said. It was an angry, sad, uneasy year. While I was in Cambridge, Jim eventually began another relationship, and although rationally I could not blame him, I felt hurt and sometimes jealous. To be torn between relationships left him embarrassed and distressed. I did not know what I wanted and neither did he. Our friends meanwhile were full of advice. Some of them thought that we needed to get this thing over and move on with our lives. Others wanted to see us back together. Yet of all the advice I heard, only this made sense to me: until we were sure what we wanted to do, we should do nothing at all.

Living alone in our house that year, I found it hard to enter the garage, Jim's woodworking shop; it made me miss him so much. I carried on by keeping myself distracted with work. I managed to finish a draft of my manuscript on Aristotle's metaphysics, even though I was also still the department chair. Then in the spring I taught an honors colloquium which I called the Literature of Spiritual Journey. It was the first time I had offered a course that was not philosophy, and imagery and the sound of words began to supplant argument in my thoughts.

Due for sabbatical, I knew I did not want to be a visiting scholar in some university's philosophy department. I did not want to have to explain what I was working on when I did not know myself. And although I no longer believed I was called to monastic life, still attracted to Grandchamp, I had begun studying French. Jim believed that his other relationship was dying, but he wanted time alone to think things through. So one winter day at 5 a.m., the hour of their noonday meal, I dialed the country code for Switzerland and Grandchamp's number. Nervously, I stumbled through the sentence I had carefully written out: "Bonjour, je voudrais parler à Soeur Maatje, s'il vous plaît." Sr. Maatje, who spoke English, was called to the phone. She warned me that their "aides" washed floors and worked in the kitchen, and I said that was just what I had in mind. I asked if, beginning in October, I could stay with them for six months.

In mid-August I found renters for our house in Fayetteville. The weather was unseasonably cool, and I commuted to the campus for a couple of weeks from a nearby state park. Camping beside a lake where I could swim was so calming that I found the courage to write potential publishers about my manuscript. Then I packed the tent and drove as far north into Ontario as there is road. One night the sky was filled with rolling clouds of light which were not clouds but only light. Despite my shivering, I stood there transfixed by the aurora borealis. A cousin of mine owns a cabin on Lake Pokegama in northern Minnesota, and I had arranged to borrow it for a month. By a most circuitous route, I arrived in Minnesota.

My cousin's cabin, before it was my cousin's, belonged to our grandfather. The site of the cabin was part of Gramps' fishing resort, where every summer of my childhood our family vacationed. What does one do with the remnants of the past? Reluctant either to get rid of Gramps' wooden rowboat or to give over the garage to it, my cousin Brian sawed the boat in two and discarded half, keeping the other half in the yard. That September, living alone in a place where time past and time present were so mingled, in the month of my mother's death, I touched my grief as gingerly as the edges of a wound. As if it were sculpture, I circled round and round the idea of her death.

I do not claim to understand what eternal life could be like although I do not see why that is necessary in order to think that life after death is possible. Had I been created before my birth and told to imagine life in this world, I would have found trying to do that perplexing too; it might be rather as picturing color for those born blind.

Of course I wish my mother and I had shared more years, and I wish my mother could have seen how women's lives have changed. But having lived most my life without her, I am accustomed to her absence. At least, that is what I was telling myself. Classical Christian theology claimed that for love of human beings to compete with love of God is sin, and St. Augustine, in the *Confessions*, believed he had grieved too much the death of a friend. I find the ideal Augustine held (but did not follow) inconceivable. I am as far from it as were our dogs. Though medieval philosophers would have thought human beings to be in some objective sense more interesting, it was Goliath that Mopsy wanted for a companion. For all the beatific vision, I cannot make myself believe that being with my mother would not matter.

The memories of my mother, they inhabit me, and I remember more than mine, for there are stories told me and there are photographs and some letters she sent to me at Girl Scout camp. But I do not have my mother, and although I continue to discover the likenesses in our lives, in a sense I do not know her, as I can only conjecture about the thought behind her actions.

While not for the too common reason of not having received a dead parent's approval (there had never been between us the sort of tension which leads mothers to send matched towels to grown daughters indifferent to housekeeping), nonetheless, it is a relationship which feels unbearably unfinished. My regard for her was never challenged by adolescence or matured by adulthood. Although I am older than my mother lived to be, I feel timelessly a child. But in truth, even had she lived longer, I doubt that the loss of her is a grief I would want to outgrow. I used to dream over and over that I would see my mother walking on a distant hill. As I began to run toward her, before I could get near, others would crowd around, and then she had to go away. God's love can be so tenacious that sometimes it seems to me God would not let creatures be unmade. Yet having lived in the unbounded emptiness of bereavement, I find it hard to hope that I will ever be with my mother.

Chapter 4

Grandchamp in October was glorious. The Jura Mountains meet the sky, and behind the monastery's wooden buildings golden trees lined the banks of the Areuse. Churning and foaming, the river rushed over even flat terrain; it was fed by mountain brooks. The name "Grandchamp" means "big field," and bordering the monastery was a field. There the farmer was harvesting his turnips. Although the work was mechanized, afterward he walked the rows with a hoe and a barrow. His cows were fenced but wore bells anyway. Their bells had a friendly sound, most of all if I walked along the river to Lake Neuchâtel at night. Spreading my parka beneath a tree, on mild afternoons I would sit close to the shore and write or think or work on French. I found I could keep warm by wearing both my sweaters.

On sunny days, across the lake the Alps were visible, the Eiger, Mönch, and Jungfrau. But most days it rained, several times, and so postcards of Switzerland deceive. I loved the rain which swelled the Areuse (though I minded the mist that held the smoke). I hoped for snow. My prayer time soon grew quiet, something that at home did not often happen, even in an empty house. Gathering for prayer, morning, noonday, evening, and before bed, the rhythms of the liturgy reflect time's syntax. By November, the trees stood stark, bare, winterized. Does all creation wait to know time's meaning?

From week to week, mail arrived from home. Tom, who in my absence served as chair, reported the revision of our graduate program. Whether to change our comprehensive exams was the most divisive question the department had faced in quite a while, and so I was grateful to Tom. He had courage I lacked. Then at 11:30 on election night, Arkansas time, I learned that Clinton would be the next President. "Cleenton, Beell Cleenton," one of the sisters whispered as we walked to morning prayer, and I ran to a newsstand in Boudry where I bought a copy of *Paris Match*. "La fabuleuse ascension de l'enfant de l'Arkansas" the cover picture of Bill and Hillary was captioned. In larger print, in English, it said, "Welcome President Clinton."

To my colleagues (and to me) in these years before the internet, it seemed that I was far away. In fact Switzerland is but one time zone beyond Cambridge, but there was the language barrier, and the idea of a monastery is itself a wall, more impenetrable than French. Late in November, the two boxes of philosophy books I had shipped to myself in August finally arrived. Just as I was moving out of our house, a journal editor had asked me to revise my paper on Plato's *Cratylus*. Then in December I learned that Cambridge University Press was interested in my manuscript on Aristotle's metaphysics.

"Lynne, what will you do when you are told to wax floors and you think there is some more important way to use your time?" Pascaline once asked when I said I was attracted to monasteries. At Grandchamp I often dreamed that I resigned my position as department chair. The winter between Cambridge and Grandchamp, at the end of a frantic week, I happened to read Merton's remarks about praying while sweeping floors and hoeing beans, and I still remember what I thought: "C'mon Merton, be real, don't give me Thoreau. What about five minutes before I teach when the phone is ringing and a graduate student waiting and I am trying to finish a letter for the secretary to type? Tell me how to feel the presence of God in the midst of that!"

The truth is that even now I mostly cannot do so. Although I believe it ought to be possible, it has not been possible for me. It is not that I experienced the presence of God in Grandchamp's laundry most mornings either. To feed the flatwork between the rollers of the stationary iron left me afterward vertiginous, a part sheered off from a machine. Yet hanging the wash and taking it down I discovered I enjoyed, and I knew the experience Merton wrote of in the peace of hauling firewood.

As for Greek philosophy, I had not wanted to think about it while I was at Grandchamp. Nonetheless, it did not seem unnatural to lay down abstract thought when the bell clanged for prayer and to take it up again at the end of a silent meal. To rewrite my paper, I needed a place where the conversations of the postulants would not distract me, nor the noise of my printer disturb anyone's prayers, and Sr. Maatje arranged for me to spread out my pages and books in an absent neighbor's lovely apartment. While Cambridge University Press was evaluating my manuscript, there was nothing I needed to do. Yet that my manuscript was being read by Cambridge I could never quite forget.

In college, Plato's eternal and unchanging Form of the Good attracted me to philosophy. That our world is an image of an imperishable Good seemed to me to make sense of this world in which the good is so breakable.

Then in graduate school, I was convinced by Aristotle's criticisms of Plato's Forms, and most of my published work has been on Aristotle. Yet *Substance and Separation in Aristotle* had been finished amid doubt not just about whether it would be published but whether the book had been worth writing. It was as if in my effort to become a professional, I somewhere lost my memory of why philosophy mattered. "If *Substance and Separation in Aristotle* is published, I would like to stay in Switzerland," I told Sr. Maatje, who was both my spiritual director and a friend. Her reply reflected my own confusion: "Lynne, there are two sides of you, and they do not fit together."

That Cambridge might publish my book pleased me and astounded me and scared me. I believed that the manuscript had some virtues, but I also knew its weaknesses, or some of them, and I knew they were faults I could not repair. More surprisingly, it was not only the inevitability of reviewers' criticism that was worrying me. Even though I could not fully explain it, the possibility of praise frightened me too. The thought of defending my view at conferences was agitating without bringing me joy. I knew I would be expected to continue to work on Aristotle, which left me feeling trapped. Nevertheless, at Grandchamp, where there were no philosophers and no writers, what was I doing? I was writing. Even as I told Sr. Maatje that I wanted to be hidden, I was attempting to find truth by tethering my experience to words.

I was writing about spiritual journey, my spiritual journey, and I knew from the care I was taking that I was writing not just for myself but for publication. Why would I, one who finds so difficult even the criticism of ideas by which philosophy proceeds, choose to expose my interior life? All that year, I fought with specious answers. Despite the role of the monasteries in medieval culture, entrenched in much monastic thought is the idea that creativity is a matter of ego, or pride, almost a kind of exhibitionism, and that troubled me inordinately. It tormented me even though it seemed not to be true.

I wanted to tell St. Benedict that the ideas and images that jumble in my mind are interior to me, but they are part of the world because I am part of the world. Words on a page are a crystallization of thought, thought that arises within me from I know not where. To write of the past is a raid on memory, and to keep my writing hidden would not repair the losses of time. Even though most books are soon out of print, I sensed that somehow I was writing in order to make my mother real, and after ordination, I understood a way in which that is true. And I saw how publishing what I have written, making it public, is part of making the act of remembering holy.

There is a much loved collect in the Book of Common Prayer that begins: "O heavenly Father, in whom we live and move and have our being." Its beautiful feminine imagery is borrowed from Acts. But if we live and move and have our being in God, then is not the consecration of the bread and wine a realization of the Real Presence, already there? By "realization" I mean in part that we become aware of God's presence in the bread and wine. But "realization" can also mean bringing about, and I intend that meaning too. I think of the Eucharist as something like incarnation; God becomes incarnate in the bread and wine. It is not so much that they come to be Other, changed in their substance, as that they have more completely the holiness that is theirs.

In the Eucharistic prayer, when the priest declares of the bread and wine, "This is my body," "This is my blood," the words and actions gather up a life past and make it present. Mere memory presumes absence, but recollection is a public and sacramental act. I believe that Christ is really, spiritually, present in the consecrated bread and wine, yet literature resonates in us too, like the Eucharist itself. Writing emerges from the unconscious, a liminal space where thought moves by symbolic equivalences, as in our dreams. To remember my mother and then write about it is to create an image of the past. But in the unconscious, past and present, representation and reality, merge.

Advent falls at the end of the university's semester, and so it is the season of final exams. At Grandchamp, as Christmas approached, for once I lived by a different calendar. The Incarnation means that God is present in Jesus and not in Jesus only. As Episcopal priest Phillips Brooks wrote in "O Little Town of Bethlehem," God is "born in us."

Meister Eckhart, a fourteenth century mystic and theologian, argued that God's ever more entering into us is not primarily a remedy for sin. It is an expression of God's nature and God's joy. Eckhart boldly described incarnation from God's point of view, and he did so with a poet's sensibility: "In this likeness or identity God takes such delight that he pours his whole nature and being into it. His pleasure is as great, to take a simile, as that of a horse, let loose to run over a green heath where the ground is level and smooth, to gallop as a horse will, as fast as he can over the greensward—for this is a horse's pleasure and expresses his nature."

Chapter 5

The late night Christmas mass was crowded, and joyous. The silence in the chapel afterward was holy, and along with members of the community, I stayed awhile into the night and prayed. I do not know what time I returned to my room to sleep, but I was awakened early Christmas morning by the sound of carols. Bearing gifts of chocolate, the postulants were singing, in English, outside my door.

Jim and I always left milk and cookies for Santa. We would decorate a Christmas tree and walk through our neighborhood just to see the Christmas lights. At Grandchamp there was no tree (and I missed it), but this was the community's way of honoring its Protestant biblical tradition. Saints were not commemorated at Grandchamp either, except those mentioned in the Bible. In Christmas week we honored the prophets Anna and Simeon. The future glory of the infant Jesus was what they foretold. Many scholars take Simeon and Anna to be the Lukan author's literary invention, but whether their historicity mattered to the community at Grandchamp I never asked. Maatje and I did not discuss biblical criticism.

For myself, I remember being disappointed when I first learned that the stories of Jesus' birth are, in all likelihood, legends. But on the other hand, even what is secular in Christmas is made sacred by its symbolic truth. Reindeer on the roof are holy messengers and tinseled trees shine with the grandeur of God. In my life, it has never been Christmas shopping, or Santa, that confuses the day's meaning. But there are other symbols, which I have sometimes failed to see as symbols. I think of my expectation of a world at peace and an idyllic family celebration.

Foolishly, I used to try to persuade Jim to go to church with me on Christmas even though the services were not luminous for him. Many years before, Christmas would heighten my stepmother's unhappiness and anger. In Bosnia, the winter I was at Grandchamp there was war, and we heard rumors of atrocities. As I write this, there is war in Afghanistan and the Sudan and Iraq and a worldwide fear of terrorism. At Christmas we sing carols to the King of Peace. But Christmas every year is shadowed somewhere by loneliness, by poverty and loss, by violence.

On Christmas morning I was missing home and friends, and most of all, I missed Jim. From the phone box outside the tram station half a mile away, nearly every week I would call him, but Christmas Day he was aboard a train to New York. Then at the festive midday meal, one of the novices said she was learning to paint icons. "I have a friend who is an icon painter," I said. Intending to express respect for her commitment and the sacred images that she makes, I added, "My friend can barely survive on what she is paid." "Icon painting is spiritual, and one must never take money for it," the novice replied.

My friend had graduate degrees and could have had a college teaching career in literature or religion or art history. By choosing to paint icons for churches, she had no health insurance. She did not know whether she would make the next month's rent. But differences in culture created a gulf too wide for either the novice's English or my halting French. Nevertheless, the misunderstanding left me frustrated and lonelier still. Even though the criticism seemed unjust, that I had been criticized brought a sense of shame. At the Christmas party later in the afternoon, as I watched that novice circling the room, her carefree bouncing step began to seem careless to me. I could not keep it from rekindling my anger.

Aristotle claimed that anything that changes must previously have been imperfect. He argued that God must not be affected by anything since being affected is a change. The stars circle because the circle is the simplest and so the best of movements. Aristotle believed their love of God causes the stars to want to be as much like God as they can. Plants and animals have offspring like themselves to imitate God, the Unmoved Mover, through vicarious eternity, yet just because God is perfect, God does not respond to their expressions of love. God thinks not of the cosmos but only of what is most worthy of thought, Aristotle argued. The only thing God thinks about is God.

St. Anselm some fourteen hundred years later gave a famous definition of God. God is, he wrote, "that than which nothing greater can be conceived." His is a definition of God that refers to perfection but does not try to describe it. In ancient and medieval Christian thought, "impassibility," that is to say, being unaffected by creation, was thought to be one of the perfections of God, but the idea was never really at home in Christianity. Because there was no room at the inn, Christ was born in a stable. The Incarnation is the surrender of control. What love brings, even for God, is vulnerability.

Chapter 5

On the ledge of Grandchamp's refectory wall, throughout the Christmas season the wise men and their camels were moved ever closer to Bethlehem. On January 6th, the Feast of the Epiphany, they reached their destination, the stable beneath the star. I wondered what the wise men left behind and to what they returned. I wondered how by their journey they were changed. By Epiphany I had been at Grandchamp almost three months. I was approaching the midpoint of my time in Switzerland.

Six months at a monastery is not anything like being in a monastery for the rest of one's life. But even three months is not a weekend either. Grandchamp was founded to reconcile the religious divisions which in Europe still remain bitter. The community was growing and had many young members and many guests. Unlike most Anglican communities in England and the States, despite the inevitable grumbling, Grandchamp was vibrant, and living in their rhythm of work and prayer, at times I found the deepest contentment I have ever known. Sometimes joy would spring up in me so strongly that I wanted to turn cartwheels across their courtyard. Joy would spring up for no reason at all.

I reveled in the silence, maintained at night, in principle (though not in fact) in the work of the day, and most of the time at meals. The surrender of authority and status was a relief, and I welcomed the end of the frantic busyness to which I was so accustomed. Yet in the absence of what the spiritual tradition calls distraction, like a kite I was buffeted by every breeze. Just as at the Christmas party, throughout my time at Grandchamp, I was flung about, again and again, by my emotions.

Living, working, and worshipping day after day, month after month, in a confined space alongside others one did not specifically choose, has some of the tensions of life in a submarine. Anxiety clung to me with a tenacity I could not loosen. Although I kept it well hidden, anger flared often, uncharacteristically so, and it did not readily subside. The monastery is a mirror for the soul, and in that mirror my fears, both those recognized and those disguised in resentment, cynicism, and inexplicable anger, stared back at me.

I went to Grandchamp supposing that I could learn some French, and by Christmas I was beginning to realize that I would not "catch on." Yet in retrospect, it was almost as if I somehow had chosen a place where I would be isolated not only by the silence, but by language. Even though I could not have articulated this at the time, the excruciating vulnerability I felt living surrounded by others and yet an outsider was a re-creation of my adolescence. In my journal I wrote that I felt like a lump in the oatmeal that wanted to be stirred into the whole. On the other hand, I was relieved to be excluded from their many community meetings. I knew I did not wholeheartedly want their communal life. For me Grandchamp was a very peculiar, inscrutable, temporarily helpful jumble. It offered a community life which I both treasured and ran from and an isolation which I both suffered from and treasured.

All the disjointed longings that are in us tend to be magnified in the Christmas season, especially Christmas in a distant place. We want to be "home" for Christmas, and we often do not know where that would be. Far from thinking that my Christmas at the monastery was a failure because it was neither glorious nor peaceful, I have come to suspect that the contrary tugs and pulls that I felt that Christmas at Grandchamp are what Christmas is really about.

Matthew's Gospel tells us that when Mary was found to be with child from the Holy Spirit, an angel appeared to Joseph in a dream. The angel said, "All this took place to fulfill what had been spoken by the Lord though the prophet: 'Look, the virgin shall conceive and bear a son and they shall name him Emmanuel,' which means 'God is with us.'" What the Nativity depicts is God's willingness to live, not removed from the turmoil, as Aristotle thought, but in the cross-purposedness and instability and limitation that characterize creation.

What is joyous about Christmas is less sorrow vanquished than creation embraced, in all its contradictions. What is joyous about Christmas is the matching of our hope to a holy birth through which our longings can be seen as signs of what created nature is yet to be. In the midst of violence and loss, when we celebrate Christmas as a season of peace and goodwill, we proclaim the end in its beginnings. Christianity proclaims that God is with us. And if God is joined with us, it is the actual human psyche in all its complexity that is joined to God.

Chapter 6

A sister rapped on my door the week I arrived at Grandchamp; to leave the shower curtain open after I had finished was "bad" ("mauvais"). The postulant next door said that at night I let the bathroom door swing shut too noisily. Working in the laundry, I had been folding the tee shirts to a size that did not fit the sisters' cupboards, and I feared there were other complaints. When I was reassigned from drying dishes to washing kettles, as if I had never washed a pot, I felt a too familiar tightening in my stomach and shoulders.

Monastic life is very rule governed, as it needs to be if many people are to live so closely together. But throughout the year the complex and unfamiliar web of expectations caused me anxiety. I remember a wintry Sunday when I had been hiking all day. Perhaps half a mile from the monastery, Sr. Jutta and Sr. Lucy Martine offered me a lift. They were in high spirits as I got into the car, putting me at ease. One of them asked if I wanted some supper, but it was 6:15 and I knew the novices would be washing dishes. Besides, I had bread and cheese left in my pack. "Would you like something to drink?" I was asked. In truth, I was thirsty and also cold, and I replied that tea would be welcome. So I followed them into the kitchen, where the tea leaves had already been dumped into the compost. Sr. Maatje offered me a grapefruit as six or so of the sisters gathered around me, not in any way unkind. Then at evening prayer that night I started silently, but very visibly, to cry.

I knew it had nothing to do with tea, whatever it was that happened. There was another place where afterward I could have made some. Nor, though I was tired and hungry, do I believe that it was my body that cried, that is to say, that it was all a matter of biochemistry rather than feelings and beliefs. The fragility I felt that night I recognized from Osage. But Osage was American and very small. When the community toured the Ozarks in their van, they made a surprise stop at the philosophy department to take me to supper, and I invited them for morning prayer and breakfast at our house. With time I had become sure, in other words, that at the doorway to their chapel I would remember to remove my shoes. More importantly, I was confident that, if I happened to forget, that too would be all right.

In Switzerland I came to see how much I depend on friendship and competence to counter fear. But later that winter something happened which I hoped might lead to change. I was making great progress reading French by then, and I was interested in the early twentieth century mystic Charles de Foucauld. Only sisters were permitted to check out books from Grandchamp's library, and so I asked Sr. Maatje if she could borrow Foucauld's essays for me. Maatje had important posts in the community, and she kept forgetting my request. Sr. Irène, my French tutor, suggested that I approach the sister in charge of the library myself. She said, "Volontiers, volontiers" which means "willingly." It is a phrase that is used like "you are welcome." So I wrote my name with the title and author and call number in the library's notebook, supposing I had permission to take the book. That was the day before Ash Wednesday.

As we prayed on Ash Wednesday, in the chapel there seemed to be an invisible but definite and powerful Presence. It gave me shape and solidity and let me feel myself a person and entitled to a place. Then the next morning the sister in charge of the library rushed up to me, not angry, but agitated, and I was so anxious that from the flow of sound which was her voice I could not extract sense. In my confusion, I kept asking her, in English, if she needed the book. After a while she managed enough English to communicate with me. The problem, I learned, was not that I had the book but rather that as librarian she needed to sign for me. Whether she could not read my signature or could not quite believe I had wanted a book written in French, or whether there was some other reason I have not thought of, what she wanted was to be sure that I was the person who had borrowed it.

That conversation ricocheted round the walls of my mind for hours afterward. I could feel the swelling in my throat, and it surprised me that I did not cry. Then suddenly I knew why. Over the years, I had read books on verbal self-defense, without effect. Yet in that conversation, in my bewilderment I somehow actually said, "But I asked beforehand!"

In Lausanne there is a museum for paintings by patients in mental hospitals. In one man's work all the human beings are portrayed as being without arms. To lack the capacity for speech in the face of threat feels like that. Being a person and the right to protest are conceptually connected, and so the sequence of events those two days was, I am certain, no coincidence. It was because of the experience on Ash Wednesday of feeling myself made solid that I held my ground.

The year I was at Grandchamp, my way of conceptualizing fear was mostly theological. I supposed the anxiety in which I lived to be unbelief. I thought that it was a failure of faith, and the fear I had of being rejected by any human being I understood as idolatry. Since God is always present, when I felt anxious or afraid, it seemed to me that I needed less to pray for awareness of God's presence than to repent. This view was supported by a story I read for my French lesson. After a pilgrim is taught by a Zen hermit to pray, the pilgrim returns to report that he can control his breathing but he has not learned to love. So the Zen master proposes a game of chess in which the winner must chop off the loser's head. The pilgrim at first plays badly. Yet eventually he is in the stronger position, and that is when he discovers he does not want to win. "You see?" says the hermit, as he pushes over the pieces: "First it is necessary to get rid of fear. Love becomes possible only after that."

I could see that those who live in fear are trouble not just to themselves. After months of trying to live in community, I could not deny that anxiety caused me to want more consideration from others than made any sense. From my experiences at Grandchamp and as department chair, I knew very well that those who too much need peace avoid issues that lead to confrontation. I could also see, by observing myself, how anxiety can bring deeper and deeper withdrawal or metamorphose into alienation.

So that winter I was forced to acknowledge how little what I say I believe and what I actually think have to do with one another. Though I believe there is a God, I knew I did not comprehend, not in the way that matters, what that really means. What it means is that, for each of us, we are welcome. What it should have meant to me was that I am accepted.

Acceptance is given not by one's mother or father (though what parents and others do helps or hinders the discovery). It is not ultimately given to me by my spouse or therapists or friends, or by philosophers or any publisher. It is not something that depends on the church or its clergy or the members of some religious order, or indeed on any human action. The source of our acceptance is God alone, and to be included in the universe is a gift from God, given to me before my mother knew she carried a child. To say as much is not meant to diminish the value of human love in our lives, but it is to admit that, even when we are not fickle in our intentions, we are too frail to be the source of one another's security. It is also to assert that, even as it is not possible, neither is it necessary. Acceptance is a gift given in creation. More exactly, since creation is an act of love, it is creation that is the gift because, in creation, acceptance is present of necessity.

When I thought this through at Grandchamp, it seemed like enlightenment to me. However, to my frustration, it was insight that did not bring lasting change. Indeed, I would now add that, although at the time I framed my fears as a failure of faith, despite all the destructive things we human beings do, repentance is a concept that often seems useless.

At Cambridge, I once visited a community on the border of England and Wales where silence had left some of its members so vulnerable that they could scarcely stand to be in the presence of one another. Another community once trusted that, if they closed out distraction, God could fill the space, and so they kept the windows boarded shut. When religious communities imposed on themselves the stresses that in solitary confinement or POW camps lead to psychological deterioration, the result was often the same. To be human is to be vulnerable, and their piety did not make them immune.

I do not mention these things because they were characteristic of Grandchamp; they were not. I mention them because, although at Cambridge I had found it incomprehensible and disillusioning that a form of life meant to bring union with God could result in psychosis, at Grandchamp it no longer seemed incredible. I came to see how easily it could happen to me. I was so out of balance. Despite the things that I had accomplished professionally, I was as far as ever from feeling secure. Locked by my lack of languages into the interior of my mind, at Grandchamp I suffered from my fear of rejection. I suffered from the extremity of my fear of criticism.

Criticism was something I would do almost anything to avoid. My fear of it was so great that being encouraged to ask for a book, or for tea, felt almost like entrapment. That there were reasons for my anxiety and that understanding those reasons could help alleviate my fears, I did not know until much later.

On Ash Wednesday at Grandchamp ashes were not imposed with the traditional words "Remember that you are dust and to dust you will return." "Return to the Lord and remember: He is tenderness and compassion" was what was said. Both are taken from verses of Psalm 103, and to me both ring true. We are returned to dust, not only at the end of our lives but, psychologically, over and over again. As for God's compassion, it did not mean that God would rescue me, not that Lent. Yet awareness of my fears had itself come to be a kind of gift, whether or not they were resolved. I had arranged to be at Grandchamp until after Easter, and I was content to stay.

Chapter 7

Every Sunday, before nine, at the Eucharist's end, I would go hiking. From midweek on, I studied the map, drawn by the romance of places not yet seen. My intention was to hike as far as I could go and still be back for evening prayer, but as, toward spring, nearby points became familiar and light lingered on the mountains, sometimes I stayed later. In Switzerland, trains run almost everywhere, and friends told me it was safe to thumb. Nevertheless I chose to tramp the Jura Mountains, all the way from the Creux du Van to Fontainemelon and into the sparsely populated valley around Sagne Eglise. I learned how treacherous the Sentiers des Quatorze Contours is when there is ice. I discovered that the way through the woods was not marked near Signal du Lessy. In the shelter which serves as a rail station for Montmollin, I saw the mural the children had painted of a round the world trip by train. Their route began in Texas and tunneled the oceans.

After a week of writing and reading, laundry and prayer, to hike was enjoyable, sheer physical exuberance. I like to be outdoors and feel the wind and sun. I liked the animals, the chamois and the wild boar that at twilight raced past me on the trail to root in the gardens of the village below. But neither curiosity nor my pent-up energy can really explain why, not just in January when the winter was mild, but in February and March, Sunday after Sunday, I kept at it. By then the footprints of farmers and foresters had disappeared like the deep-buried path itself. Yet in woods unmarked by tracks of even snowshoes and skis, on gray days I trudged through knee-deep snow toward some arbitrary distant point, a name marked on my map.

It must partly have been habit. Even when I had a cold, I kept going. It did not matter if my feet were wet despite good boots and my fingers numb from having taken off my gloves to fumble with my camera or my pocket-knife and bread and cheese. Certainly I cannot claim that I was thinking, though fragments of French and Taizé chant ran sometimes through my mind. But more important than any thoughts I could have had were those that mile by mile I forgot. It is hard to live in community. In places where people can generally be counted on to be kind, it is an irony that events which might, in another context, be all but unnoticed too often become the focus of attention. However, even when the week had been harmonious, constant proximity was for me a cause of fatigue. Walking, I slipped from solitude to loneliness and back and back again as easily as the clouds slid past a distant ridge, yet in hiking I found peace. The uphill slow plod and the pounding down were repair.

Over the months, and hills, I watched, as weather and the season, or even my direction, could recreate the landscape. Playing tag with rain or snow or sleet, by fog I was often captured, and I sometimes chased the sun. Once on a hillside bare of snow I lay down and fell asleep. I never knew how Grandchamp was on Sundays, but whatever I missed was less important than what I found. I unfailingly returned content with the community and with myself. Just as the journey of the chamois is the journey of the chamois and the journey of the black pig running in the twilight at the end of winter or the beginning of spring belongs to the black pig, so I rejoiced that my journey was mine.

As spring brought my time at Grandchamp to a close, I had many memories. There was Holy Week; on Palm Sunday a neighbor's donkey, borrowed for the procession, was tied outside the chapel where it began to bray every time we chanted. Most of the community took a leisurely walk into the Jura on Holy Monday, stopping at improvised stations of the cross to pray. On Good Friday we laid flowers at the "tomb of Jesus" in the chapel and prayed for the state of the world. Holy Saturday was a day of unbroken silence, and on Easter the chapel was crowded with guests, one of whom was my friend Cintra from St. Helena's in the States. Cintra and I had last met in England, and it was she who first suggested that I visit Grandchamp. Cintra was almost the only American I saw at Grandchamp all year.

Chance brought friendships of the moment with other visitors. One of these was Elsa, a Little Sister of Jesus from Einsiedeln, near the Austrian border, who came to Grandchamp twice that spring. Elsa spoke English, and as we washed dishes, she told me about Charles de Foucauld, who inspired her religious order. Foucauld lived as a hermit in the North African desert and ventured forth to help the nomadic tribes. In World War I, he was killed as a spy. Before returning to the States, I would visit Elsa in Einsiedeln, where in the fields I saw magnificent horses, like the Lipizzaner stallions. I watched the crowds praying before the Black Madonna in the cathedral at Einsiedeln. Einsiedeln was a place of pilgrimage, not tourism, and the crowds were reverent.

Another week I was privileged to have a conversation with Canon A.M. (Donald) Allchin, then an assistant to the Archbishop of Canterbury. I admire his book *Participation in God: A Forgotten Strand in Anglican Tradition*. The forgotten strand is *theosis*; God takes on our human nature in the Incarnation so that we might participate in the divine. And I attended lectures on Irenaeus given to the community by a monk visiting from Taizé. Even though he lectured in French, to everyone's surprise, I was able to comprehend most of what he said. But more than all the visitors, after my departure, it was the community I would remember.

Grandchamp's laundry was itself an education. The place seemed always to be the hub for chatter, so much so that in the supposed silence of Lent, one day I skipped the noonday prayers in order just to sit beneath a tree. Another week someone washed the beautiful white linen tablecloths together with red rags for mopping the floors. Dismayed, I asked the postulant in charge of the laundry why the floor rags had to be red and was told that red was Sr. Monique's favorite color. "So why not put up a sign asking everyone to separate red laundry from white?" I asked. "No one reads signs," Marion said.

Even though my grasp of written French far exceeded my facility with speech and I was always reading signs, in a multilingual community, I could see the point of Marion's reply. When she had rejected all my suggestions, I shrugged and said, "Life is complex," and she replied, "No, it isn't." The idea that human life has, or at least should have, a kind of unity and simplicity is a monastic truism, yet it is a truism that to me does not ring true. Even if, as many saints have said, our deepest desire is always for God, our shared desire for God does not provide much practical guidance for our common life. As long as some human beings find God in care given to laundry and others in detachment from it, they will disagree about the importance of keeping white linen tablecloths white.

The color of floor rags matters. The beauty of color images the beauty of God and so can mediate a desire for God. In fact, our desires often carry layer upon layer of mediating meanings, which can be obscure even to ourselves. When it fell to me to iron the pajamas of the head of the community (no one else's were ironed), I resented it, and I attributed the resentment I felt to egalitarian ideals. In retrospect, I think what I was feeling was more like the contempt I had in college for peers who were still close to their parents. By labeling the feelings of my classmates "immaturity," I did not have to admit that I wanted a family to which I could feel close.

The desire for God can be mediated even by our misinterpretations of one another. I remember the time Isabelle left me a note about the noise I made at night closing the bathroom door. It happened to be my monthly retreat day, and I did not want to spend hours struggling with French. "Je vais essayer" ("I will try") was as long a reply as I could write without consulting a dictionary and grammar. But I discovered afterward that the postulants admired me for what they took to be the simplicity of my response. I was angry, yet to the postulants who struggled with their own emotions, I symbolized "the joy and peace of the journey." Not seeing my internal turmoil, they concluded that years of contemplative prayer had made me nondefensive and calm.

A few weeks later, on my 45th birthday, I was alone, folding clothes, when Sr. Michèle, the novice mistress, came into the laundry. There seemed to me a gentleness and luminosity about Sr. Michèle that always drew me to her, but she knew as little English as I did French. As she left she said, "Merci pour les belles choses" ("thank you for the beautiful things") and something in her manner suggested she was not referring to clean laundry. Afterward, one of the novices stopped by and said, "You look very happy. Is it a special day?" and I replied that it was my birthday even though Michèle's puzzling words were the cause of my joy. Then Psalm 45, my age, was sung at evening prayer to acknowledge my birthday, and to my surprise, someone left flowers in a small jar at my door.

The Sunday after Easter, Sr. Maatje drove me to my train in Neuchâtel although I could easily have got there by tram. When she asked me to call her before I left Europe, I could see that she was having as much trouble saying goodbye as I was, and to know that made me glad. But I grieved even more saying goodbye to Sr. Irène. Twice weekly I had knocked at Sr. Irène's door for my French lesson and she would sing out "Entrez!" Taking my hands, she always exclaimed that they were cold. Sr. Irène had been a Girl Scout, as had I, and she remembered the trails of the Jura. In Grandchamp's early days, she had hung the clothes outside and run to take them down each time it rained. With Irène I shared my photographs; to her I read the Psalms. One day she asked me about my grandmothers and, learning I did not know them, she declared herself my "French Grandmother." Two years after I left Grandchamp, Maatje wrote to tell me Sr. Irène had died.

At Grandchamp, I often could not sleep as bits of French darted like fish through the ocean of incomprehension. I would have liked to walk around, but the walls between the rooms did not dampen sound. My shoes would have thundered like the feet of elephants on the wooden stairs. At the New Year's party, Sr. Michèle greeted me as "Soeur Lynne," words I doubted I had heard rightly until at my departure, in a card that began in English and ended in French, she repeated them. In Easter week, I was asked to supper with the postulants. This was their way of inviting me to stay. Then the night before I left, Sr. Philomena claimed that my departure was not permitted by their rule, in other words, by the document that governed their life. To Grandchamp I had backpacked fear; it was as real as books and clothes. But in the mock coercion of an eighty year old nun, I clearly heard love, and I could not contain my laughter.

Chapter 8

The Feast of St. Anselm on April 21, 1993, marked the 900th anniversary of Anselm's becoming a bishop. In the year 1093 he set out for Canterbury from his monastery at Bec in Normandy. One day I asked Sr. Johanna, one of Grandchamp's novices, if she got letters from her friend Sr. Stephanie. Stephanie was a novice at Bec who stayed at Grandchamp for a while. Together she and I had waxed the floors. In many religious orders, correspondence with novices is restricted, and so when Johanna proposed I write to Stephanie myself I was surprised. Because the Episcopal Church is part of the Anglican Communion, Stephanie invited me to Bec for the celebration.

It was something of a busman's holiday to go to Bec. Upon leaving Grandchamp, I had intended to be a tourist, and from Bec I did travel to Bayeux and Mont St. Michel, then south to the Pyrenees and across Provence. But for a few days first, I walked along the road where St. Anselm thought and prayed, and I listened to Gregorian chant sung gloriously at the Abbey.

One might assume Sr. Stephanie's invitation delighted me. It should have. But I knew there would be Church of England officials there, and I still travel like a student with a backpack and in jeans. I feared I would feel out of place, and I had heard rumors about the arcane etiquette observed at Bec at meals. Yet even in the midst of my anxiety, something in me argued that such things should not count. And besides, I remembered that, unlike Grandchamp, at Bec guests would eat in the guesthouse, away from the community. So I accepted the invitation, and at Bec I found that all the scenes I had played out in my mind existed only there. The guesthouse was noisy. After months at Grandchamp the transition was so jarring that when I was invited to take my meals in silence with the community, I accepted gratefully. I chose the very arrangement the thought of which had almost kept me from going, and it turned out fine. At the beginning of my first meal in their refectory, the abbess washed my hands, yet I did not feel embarrassed. It seemed that Grandchamp had been good for me.

I traveled around France for a month before returning to Fayetteville. I had visited Paris once before, but that time I had not been able to explore the French countryside. This trip gave me a sense of France's history and its regions. I still remember the magnificence of the Bayeux tapestry and the vividness with which it presents medieval life. Our longing for God is mirrored in the inaccessible beauty of Mont St. Michel, as it sits atop the rocks of what is an island at high tide. Following the path of medieval pilgrimage to Santiago de Compostelo, I hiked the arid landscape of the Pyrenees almost to the border of Spain, and I watched the light, so loved by the Impressionist painters, play upon the fields in Provence. I often asked myself where I was going, and I had few answers. Nevertheless, I was ready to go home. When I finally arrived in Fayetteville, almost the first thing I did was to trade cars.

Returning from Grandchamp, where for six months, apart from bread and cheese for hiking, I hardly entered a shop, it was an incongruous decision. It was even more so as my subcompact was running well enough. Yet having resided in Europe two of the previous three years, our house no longer seemed to be the place where I lived. I intended to visit Osage Monastery often and, I hoped, Jim in Illinois. I had come to think of myself as a nomad, and I wanted to feel at home in my car.

I was not oblivious to the environment even then. I have always ridden my bicycle to school. Nevertheless, I thought a heavier vehicle would be better suited to the speed of the highways, and I wanted a car with air conditioning and more cargo space and four-wheel drive. So I emptied my savings account and cashed my last travelers' checks. Then I bought a year old Jeep.

Technology often baffles me. When I turned on the ignition and saw the message flash "check engine," I did not realize it was the signal itself that was being checked. The cruise control, which I was too timid to try on the test drive, turned out not to work. When the speedometer began to waft meaninglessly, the salesperson assured me it would be fixed, but a few weeks later it began to waft again. In the middle of the night I found myself muttering, "Someone tell me God does not require that I be good at trading cars."

To suppose that at 24000 miles I might be experiencing the beginning of its disintegration made me so anxious that I wanted to push the Jeep off a cliff and out of my life. Instead, unable to sleep, I, who am seldom histrionic, walked into the garage and chalked a rectangle around my Jeep, ordering it to stay there, away from the bedroom if it wanted to live with me. Then, unable to remain angry with such a beautiful vehicle, I pleaded, "Look, Jeep, it is just that I can't let you take the place of God." Of course, it was not the Jeep which was disturbing my sleep. My sleeplessness was due to Jeep-thoughts, and my Jeep-thoughts were in me. Besides, I did not know: would I have preferred my money back and my tiny Ford Festiva without air conditioning, if they were offered me?

How much I missed Grandchamp when I bought the Jeep that summer! Having to bargain left me reeling. Assuming I had been lied to about the speedometer, I thought I had been robbed. I was mad at the dealership and mad at myself for hurrying into a decision. More than that, the Jeep collided with the hub of my madness by compelling me to live with uncertainty. I knew my bank balance was insufficient to cover whatever might go wrong. I am terrified of the unfixable, and I grieve the broken; indeed, I always have. Yet at Grandchamp when the washing machine died in Holy Week, I had no responsibility about its replacement, and in fact, none of the sisters made such decisions alone. Why had I chosen to come back?

There is a view which I once held. It is that if one wants simplicity and a life centered on God, the world is an impossible place to live. After all, even Thoreau went to the woods when he wished to live deliberately. He said he wanted to front only the essential facts of life and see if he could not learn what it had to teach so that, when he came to die, he would not discover he had not lived. We think of Thoreau's building his cabin. We remember his hoeing beans. Yet Thoreau was writing one of the classics of American literature at Walden Pond. He was reading Homer in Greek and urging others to do the same. And just as Thoreau went to the woods in order to study life itself, so for the same reason he left. Thoreau moved away from Walden Pond after two years.

When Pascaline and I were talking at Osage Monastery about religious orders, one day she warned me: "Lynne, in men's orders there can be writers; women peel potatoes." In fairness, it must be said that there are exceptions, yet in contemplative orders in Europe, this did seem to be the norm. The year I was in England, the mother superior of Burnham Abbey told me not to bother to visit. In her letter she implied I would be bored.

To work in Grandchamp's laundry writing about working in the laundry softened my experience of working in a laundry. Whenever I met God in folding socks, the encounter was clothed in creativity; I was meeting words, images, whole sentences. However, by spring the truths whispered by the socks were only about socks, and the jeans no longer fashioned into words as they were folded. Most of all, I missed Jim, and I missed friends.

At Grandchamp I carried the beatitudes in the pocket of my jeans because they were sometimes recited as part of the noonday office. I kept the French, "heureux ceux qui sont purs en leur coeur," "blessed are the pure in heart," ready-to-hand. In monastic tradition, purity of heart is to be found by paring down possessions and speech and inessential work. It is found by limiting the intimacy of human relationships.

That God is to be found by subtraction is an idea that runs deep in classical thought, both pagan and Christian. In the *Enneads* the third century pagan Neoplatonist Plotinus proposed this as a spiritual exercise: "Let there be, then, in the soul a shining imagination of a sphere, having everything within it, either moving or standing still, or some things moving and others standing still. Keep this, and apprehend in your mind another, taking away the mass: take away also the places, and the mental picture of matter in yourself..." St. Augustine was influenced by Plotinus, and in the *Confessions* he recorded that, shortly before his mother's death, he and his mother shared a vision. "If to any man the tumult of the flesh grew silent, silent the images of earth and sea and air: and if the heavens grew silent, and the very soul grew silent to herself and by not thinking of self mounted beyond self: if all dreams and imagined visions grew silent, and every tongue and every sign and whatsoever is transient," then, wrote Augustine, it is possible "to touch the eternal Wisdom which abides over all."

For both Plotinus and Augustine, the task was to still the self and turn from the many and the changing to the One, from the temporal to the Eternal, and in fact during Holy Week at Grandchamp, my friend Cintra said that living there had given me a remarkable interior unity. But if that was true, it did not last. In Fayetteville, I knew that I would have to discover whether awareness of God and complication can coexist.

Stories about Zen masters whose enlightenment causes them to return to the world are plentiful, but I had not reached enlightenment. For Kierkegaard, the knight of faith leads a life that is indistinguishable from that of his neighbors, but I will never be a knight of faith. Simone Weil's "Reflections on the Right Use of School Studies with a View to the Love of God" I have found useful. Weil argued that the solution to a geometry problem, an example of a particular truth, is an image of Christ, the eternal and living Truth. She claimed that the soul that empties itself in order to receive into itself a truth of geometry is learning to attend absolutely to God and just as absolutely to human suffering.

In Weil's view, attention is what makes experience a school for learning to love God. But I wonder: is God also experienced in distraction, or is distraction, by definition, a failure to experience whatever is most significant? And what is it that we label distraction, and why? Classical culture thought of multiplicity as a falling away from unity, but is it so? Is multiplicity necessarily distraction? That summer the thoughts I took to be distractions were during prayer as agile as cats. They still are.

Chapter 9

The heat of the August day had vanished. It fled into the night, like the sound of two guitars when the concerto reached its end. I-57 was uncrowded, but I had followed the taillights of the van in front of me through so many miles that it was as if the Jeep were being towed. The flat midwestern landscape let my mind drift back in time to night road trips long ago. Then I would lie wrapped in a blanket on the back seat of our Dodge. Comfortable and half-asleep, I would listen to the murmur of my parents' conversation. Often my mother would be driving. She liked to drive at night. I cannot think of anything about her without remembering: my mother did not live.

Two days earlier I had no reason to suppose I would be driving to Illinois. As I lay on the examining table, uncomfortably bloated, a technician, with the sort of seriousness from which one can conclude nothing, asked me to wait, and soon doctors were hovering over me. They wanted to see for themselves the echo produced image of a mass they thought too gray to be an ovarian cyst.

The radiologist intended to call my doctor that afternoon, but she was out of town, as was my therapist. St. Paul's new priest had not arrived, and after two years abroad, it seemed that all my friends lived elsewhere. Jim offered straightaway to drive to Fayetteville. But knowing he had work to finish, for he had unexpectedly spent half the summer in New York while his mother was ill, I proposed that I go to his place for the weekend instead. Meanwhile (this was a Thursday), I went to the office and caught up on paperwork. On Friday at noon, Jim and I exchanged phone calls, twice. Trying to be rational about a trip that took at least ten hours, we decided that, until we knew what was going to happen, we should both stay where we were.

Then unpacking my half packed duffel bag in a suddenly too empty house, I picked up the phone and said, "I'm on my way."

There are some things in life that thoughts of death knife through. I had been to Illinois soon after returning from Switzerland. That weekend Jim and I had cruised around Crystal Lake Park at five miles an hour listening to Wagner over the Jeep's four speakers, but between marriage and divorce we did not decide. The specter of illness did not settle it either, yet the question was shelved and elsewhere clarity came. Never mind that it was joined with "rare and improbable," "something that simply has to be ruled out," the day I heard the word "cancer," I did not send to Lands' End for flannel shirts as I intended, mine being too worn to wear to school, nor did I respond to the APA dues notice on my desk or register for French. Yet after a few days, I began to rethink how to live in the indefinite.

The idea, it seemed to me, was to continue in the ordinary routines of life as if there were time and in relationships as if there were not. If I became abrupt with some person in the payroll office because the sick leave on my paycheck said "eight hours" instead of the hundreds I knew I must have accumulated, when would I undo having made the world worse? It quickly became clear that things that felt unfinished, most of all, my relationship with Jim, mattered more than medical reports. And I knew I had also to make peace with philosophy.

I admire Socrates. I admire him for the keenness of his mind and, more than that, for the interior freedom which, during his trial on charges of impiety and corrupting the youth of Athens, let him conduct his defense exactly as he wished. Even so, I understand the mixed responses of students. "Pressing his opponents into contradiction was his way of teaching them." "No, he didn't help anyone; he just embarrassed them," students argue. I remember an honors student who so despised him for his rudeness and his arrogance that she refused to go on reading. In the opening scenes of the *Protagoras*, Plato wrote that, seeing Socrates and his friend in the doorway, the porter shouted, "Sophists!" Then, in order to keep them out, he slammed the door as hard as he could with both hands.

My first year in graduate school, being new to philosophy, I was so overwhelmed that I had no time to ask myself if I liked what I was doing. The second year, I returned because I could live on my assistantship and had no idea what I would do instead. Then that winter I was, to my surprise, offered a fellowship. By then I was enjoying most of my classes, and besides, I did not want to leave Urbana-Champaign because I had fallen in love with Jim. To be writing a dissertation I found exciting. I argued (persuasively, I still think) that fatalism about future events rests on a confusion between thinking about time simply as one event's being later than another, a relationship which is static or unchanging, and time as a flowing stream. I was proud of what I had written, and I thought philosophy was where I belonged. But after ten years or so in Arkansas, the doubts I had early in graduate school came back.

For me, it is not Socrates who seems just too abrasive. Even if his manner is arrogant, what he has to say is not. At his trial Socrates told the jurors the oracle proclaimed no one to be wiser than he because he recognized that only the gods know anything worthwhile. I think Socrates really did value truth above all else. He understood philosophy to be the means to it and a divinely imposed mission. We do need to reflect on what it is to be human and how we should live our lives, just as Socrates claimed. Socrates thought there was truth to be known and that we ought to persevere. He held nothing to be as worthwhile as the search for knowledge.

On the other hand, when I first encountered A.J. Ayer's *Language, Truth, and Logic*, a source of the logical positivist view that only the empirically verifiable is meaningful, I was outraged. I was so frustrated at having no rejoinder that I cried. It is odd that after the demand for verification had been abandoned in other areas of philosophy, it persisted in the philosophy of religion, and as a graduate student, after a while I came to think it a reasonable demand. Indeed I had so internalized the heavy-handed requirements for evidence and clear argumentation that once at St. Martin's I told Bill that philosophy was the arbiter of the meaningful. "Have a little humility," Bill laughed. Then, as meditating stirred my longing for the transcendent, I began to find philosophy deadening. I had entered philosophy thinking it would satisfy my longing for Truth, and it seemed instead that I had starved.

In Plato's account of Socrates' death, Socrates was told in his dreams to write poetry. One of the most significant philosophers of the twentieth century was Heidegger, and in his late writings, as a model for philosophy, he turned to art. Yet contempt for Heidegger was in my graduate student days a commonplace, and I did not have the independence of mind to question it. In the analytic philosophy of my years in graduate school, all that was literary in Plato was at best decorative and at worst an impediment. As a teacher, I have found that what is taught and what is learned are not always the same. I am describing only what I learned. It seemed to me that the exaltation of words was joined to a view of what is the right and proper thing to be done with them. I saw it as the assertion of a way of thinking, writing, and valuing that had no patience with poetry or ambiguity, and I uncritically supposed that "contemporary" meant "most advanced."

"Philosophy" seemed to have given me a set of standards not just for how to do philosophy but for what was worth doing. A voice within me was telling me that the writing I had begun to do at Grandchamp was worthless, just because it was "literary," and since the judgment I was hearing was my own, I could not dismiss the charge. I feared that my writing would embarrass my colleagues, and I knew that I would feel exposed. One day shortly after my return from Europe, I heard myself mutter, "If I were dying, I would write what I want!" Only weeks later, the ultrasound was taken.

In a much reprinted dialogue about personal identity and immortality written for students, contemporary philosopher John Perry made use of science fiction to test our intuitions. In Perry's imagined world, just as there are heart transplants and kidney transplants, so the brain can be transplanted into another human body. In the dialogue, a philosopher who has been rushed to the hospital after a motorcycle accident that has irreparably damaged other vital organs, but not her brain, discusses a brain transplant with some friends. Her friends urge her to let her brain be transplanted, arguing that not to do so could even be considered suicide. The dying philosopher argues that she is her body, a living human body; if her brain were transplanted to another body, she would not be the one who survived. The conversation ends with her death, and the issue does not reach resolution.

"That is not what it is like to watch someone's dying," some years ago a student protested. Annoyed, I brushed off the student's response by telling him that in Perry's dialogue the scene was just a setting for the arguments, which were the only thing that mattered. Then after I returned from Grandchamp, I became distressed about how I had treated that student years before. Belatedly, I wondered whose death he had been grieving.

I blamed Perry's dialogue for being remote and impersonal. In my memory, it came to seem flippant in its treatment of human relationships, and for a long time I did not teach the dialogue because I did not want students to suppose that it showed how philosophers think human beings should be. Then, some years afterward, I reread the dialogue and saw it so differently that I assigned it again. Perry's dialogue was not meant to address the existential realities of dying or of grieving; it is about the conditions for identity. Nevertheless, my irritability had been telling me something, something true. What I had failed to see was that the truth it told was not about Perry's dialogue. And it was not about philosophy.

Chapter 10

Jim went with me to Little Rock for the surgery. The only way to test for ovarian cancer was to remove the ovary. The surgeon recommended that I have both ovaries removed and also a hysterectomy, but unwilling to take hormones, I did not agree to that. Fayetteville and Little Rock are separated by almost two hundred miles, and I thought I would not know anyone, which turned out not to be true. Joyce, once a deacon at St. Paul's, lived there.

She met us at the hospital, and the three of us talked of movies when the pre-op was over. Afterward, as I lay hooked to the intravenous mechanism in the holding room for more than two hours, Jim and I exhausted every subject from football to Greek philosophy that we could think of. It was how we kept fear at the end of the hall. I asked him to make the final changes in my manuscript for Cambridge, if it came to that.

The anesthesiologist stopped by and said he once had a philosophy course. His instructor at Hendrix College was someone I knew. The number of philosophers in Arkansas is small. When at last the surgeon arrived, beneath lights brighter than a TV studio's, the anesthetic was started. The next thing I remember is that Jim told me the findings. I fell back to sleep, awakened by surreal dreams every fifteen minutes throughout the night. I was grateful to be alive. And it had not been cancer.

Some days later, when Jim had to return to Illinois, I thought I could manage. But after several weeks of walking around the summit of Fayetteville's Mt. Sequoyah, an easy walk that kept me close to my car, the view seemed too familiar. So I ventured forth toward the campus instead, which was a mistake. My intention was to turn around after thirty minutes, but just when the distance was greatest, pain and fatigue made me unwell. I like the neighborhood alongside Wilson Park, old brick or stone and frame houses, big trees, small yards, the quiet streets of a quieter decade. Through the undraped windows I could see couples moving from room to room, doing the things that in early evening families do. I should have knocked on a door, any door, and asked if someone could call a cab. Instead, I leaned against my hiking staff and rested on a low stone wall, and then walked on still more slowly.

At the end of the street, outside the local hospital there were people milling about. Though it was past time for changing shifts, a nurse's aide was headed toward her car. She was young and looked approachable, and I wanted to ask her for a lift. By then I was only six blocks from home, but four of them were straight uphill. It would not, I said to myself, be much out of her way, whatever her direction, and she would surely understand. But still I did not do it.

I wondered while I walked why I decided as I did. Yet it was just the sort of decision I too often make. Before I left Grandchamp, I admitted to Sr. Maatje that my small room contained a three-foot high heap of used computer paper, a six month accumulation which was there because I had been reluctant to ask anyone how to dispose of it. And that habit, which even at Grandchamp kept me more an outsider than was necessary, after surgery became pernicious. My fear of rejection (or of assistance given in a way that lets me know I have imposed) got joined with anger that help had not been given when in fact it was not asked. Watching cars go past me as I struggled up the hill, I could not pretend I did not know my feelings of being neglected, ignored, and uncared for would make asking the next time an even steeper climb. I knew that I was slipping into depression.

I have always been physically fit, and so I naturally assumed recovery would go easily. For the first week or so after surgery, it seemed that it would. Then in the midst of pain, unexplained nausea, and fatigue, I returned, probably too soon, to teaching. As I fought for concentration to revise my manuscript for Cambridge, recovery seemed so slow I feared it would not occur at all. I was angry at a body that did not work. Mortality, my mortality, became as real to me as the hospital bracelets I had not thrown away. The calm which in the weeks before surgery enabled me to sort through medical options and all the intricacies of insurance coverage disappeared, and I began to second-guess my decision not to have a hysterectomy. I have heard people say that to them God feels nearest when they are most in need, but when I am in trouble, my awareness of God vanishes.

I was puzzled and ashamed that, so soon after returning from Grandchamp, I could be attacked by depression. I did not even have cancer. Yet time had circled; the past was more real than the present. My mother's death and my strained relationship with my father and stepmother in the years that followed seemed to make all relationship impossible. It was as if being motherless had left me unable to be part of the human community, and since the past is unchangeable, it did not seem that anything could change. In a sense, the aftermath of surgery let me find the very thing I went to the monastery seeking, but in finding it, I was lost. I felt totally alone, and yet my relationship with my mother must have left some trace of trust because I started over in therapy that autumn. I knew I needed to talk about my mother's death.

The night after her death, I had stayed with the family of my best friend because my room was needed for my uncle and aunt. I arrived at my friend Rita's house in time for supper, during which the conversation was casual. I was still wondering if Rita knew (no one had said anything) while she and I watched TV. Finally at bedtime Rita announced, "My mother wants me to give you this." Her family was Christian Scientist, but her mother must have gone shopping at a Catholic bookstore. I concluded that my friend knew when, in embarrassed silence, she handed me a portrait of Jesus that glowed in the dark.

As my father and grandfather and aunts and uncles and I visited the mortuary, my idea of what it would be like came from a movie. My mother was usually very careful about what movies I saw, but she once sent a visiting cousin and me to see the only movie playing within walking distance of our house. Even though I knew my mother would be clothed and in a coffin, I thought we would search for her through rooms filled with rows of coffins. I believed it would be like the search for Spartacus among the battlefield's dead.

The next day during the funeral, certain that adults do not cry, I did not cry. About the funeral I remember almost nothing else. Nevertheless, I am sure I have within me some unconscious memory of the closing of the coffin and its being carried from the church. As the coffin was slid into the hearse and the door closed, the door to my life was also being locked.

After the funeral relatives scattered to their homes, hundreds of miles away. My mother was rarely mentioned by anyone, including me, and after a time, I felt almost violated if she were spoken of. Glow-in-the-dark-Jesus smiled above my bed in what seemed to me serene indifference. No doubt the death of a young mother stirred everyone's fears of mortality, and few in the church or neighborhood seemed to know what to do or say. Some weeks after the funeral my homeroom teacher did ask me how things were going. She happened to be a teacher we kids all despised, and I told her things were fine. As for my new classmates, I hardly knew them, but (so far as I could tell) they all had mothers. I desperately did not want to be different, but still I was different. One day I had a mother and the next glow-in-the-dark-Jesus hung on my wall. I sensed I lived with something they could not begin to comprehend.

Even as I recovered from ovarian surgery, I was making frequent trips to Omaha. Both my father's and stepmother's health failed that winter, and after my stepmother's death and Dad's move to assisted living, I ransacked the basement and attic of the house. The green glass flower vase, a wicker picnic basket, the cotton blanket with blue covered wagons around its border, everything that had belonged to my mother, I lugged back to Fayetteville. I took her high school diploma and textbooks from x-ray training. I took her Bible and old greeting cards, some she had written and never sent, some I had made for her. I even found a metal box of slides.

I had never seen pictures from our vacation that last summer, a vacation cut short when she became too ill to go on. The twelve year old in pony tails and saddle shoes, who was almost as tall as I am now but skinny, stood happily beside her as she posed with us kids beneath Babe the Blue Ox in Bemidji. Retrieving my mother's belongings from the hidden recesses of the house was a way of grieving, but in keeping these bits and tatters of my mother's life, there was also a stubborn assertion. My mother lives in my memory, but that does not mean I just imagined that she existed. In my hand I could hold a Christmas card she wrote.

I have been asked, what is the point of it, the awareness of childhood's pain? Of course the question—why would one want awareness?—presumes that there is choice. Contemplative prayer had invited me into myself, but after surgery, I did not choose. Memory was like a river, like a flood.

It was in the spring semester of that academic year that I taught the honors colloquium on the Literature of Spiritual Journey (broadly understood). I did it because I was tired of Introduction to Philosophy and wanted to read writers who cared about their prose. We read classics like *Walden* and St. Augustine's *Confessions*, as well as more recent works like *Zen and the Art of Motorcycle Maintenance* and May Sarton's *Journal of a Solitude*. I told the students that I wanted them to think about their own lives and to do some autobiographical writing, some they would share with one another, some for me. About halfway through the term, one of them asked if I would read something of mine to them, and so I read a short piece in which I told them of my mother's death and how finding myself so alone in junior high colored my experience of Grandchamp. I told them that I learned at Grandchamp how I still struggle to accept acceptance.

Maybe it mattered to them to know that their professor's adolescence had not gone easily, but I got to know that group of students in a way that went beyond their ability to do philosophy or write good prose. I discovered that some of them had lives that were more troubled than I ever imagined. I can wonder whether my role in encouraging their self-knowledge in early adulthood was wise, and though the students praised the course, I have never taught it again. Yet I do know that at the right time the remembrance of suffering has purpose.

To attempt to express compassion without knowledge of one's own pain increases the isolation of another. To discover that suffering is universal, on the other hand, diminishes shame. One week when my therapist told me to read a story in which a dying mother gives her daughter a doll, I brought to her office the Raggedy Ann my mother made for me. As we talked, I watched her holding my doll. She was arranging her limbs, smoothing her yarn hair, and straightening her dress. We are vulnerable to one another, much more than we ever know. What is the point of the remembrance of childhood's pain? Here is one answer: the awareness of our own lives helps us be trustworthy with trust.

Chapter 11

It startled me to see my stepmother hunched over in a wheelchair in the nursing home. Amy was mumbling and confused, yet oriented enough to be perplexed that I was there. That evening Dad asked me to accompany her when she was rushed to the hospital emergency room. I had brought my developmentally disabled brother Ed to Omaha with me. Dad said he would stay with Ed.

Lonely and incapable of managing the household, my father remarried only six months after Mother's death. Our new stepmother was a close friend of my mother's who had always been kind to us kids. Yet even though to relatives and neighbors and friends the arrangement seemed ideal, Amy's moods soon began to swing, unpredictably, between extremes of generosity and anger. When sometimes for days she refused to speak, the slam of her bedroom door announcing a silence more incisive than speech, my panicked father would take me aside and in a whisper tell me that, because of something I had done, or failed to do, Amy did not feel welcome. He would tell me that I had to make things right.

I can remember how much I hated being made to wear high heels and nylons and dresses. I remember that I could not see why I needed to mend my cotton panties just because they had holes. Once I carelessly left the freezer door open, and the matter never died. Another time my stepmother found and read my diary, and I sulked. At night I counted down the years, then the months, until college. But when it came, rather than feeling free fifty miles away, I actually became more anxious. Their visits unpredictable, I would approach the dorm circuitously. I wanted to avoid being seen while I checked whether their Chrysler was there.

On a campus of 17000, it would have been easy for me to disappear whenever their car was present. Yet knowing they would berate me, instead I braced myself. I would get in the car with them and let it happen. It was not as if I had smoked pot. I did not even drink or smoke. I had not discovered sex. Neither was I, I half regret to say, standing with those who carried placards protesting the war. I was working in the cafeteria, practicing the piano, going to class and making A's. I was, by common measures, a "good kid." What was it that so agitated my family? My roommate, an art major, was convinced I would look pretty if I let my hair grow long, and I would not cut my hair.

I realize now that books and college and classical music, all things outside his experience, made my father ill at ease. I know that my inner life left my stepmother insecure. And I can conjecture that both were deflecting toward me some of the tensions in their marriage. To my dad and stepmother, long hair was enough at that time to make me a hippie. Nevertheless, many years later, when my brother Doug said to me, "I was brought up to be *not like you*," I was so astounded that I asked him why they had hated me. My youngest brother is a research chemist and a levelheaded guy. I thought he would tell me I was exaggerating. Instead he replied, "Lynne, it was just that you were there."

I was thinking about all these things, and more, the winter that followed my surgery. Looking back, I could see a tragic collision of fantasies. I desperately wanted Amy to be a mother to me, and I just as emphatically did not want it. Amy once told me that Dad would have put us kids in foster care had she not married him, which unsettled me, yet it might have been true. But even as Dad remarried to have a mother for his children, he also wanted a mother for himself. As for Amy, it seems that she married my father because she was attracted to three year old Doug and to an ideal of family life which could never be fulfilled. Unfortunately, divorce was unthinkable among their acquaintances. And finally there was Ed, whose presence inevitably produced enormous tension. Surely it was ironic that, even as I was in therapy discovering how angry I was, I was also driving back and forth to Omaha to attend to my stepmother and my dad.

It was a Saturday night when Amy was rushed to the hospital. The emergency room was full of injured children and victims of accidents. An old woman with an erratic heart beat could hardly be the staff's priority. So when Amy complained of being cold, although I asked for a blanket and someone said "Sure," no one came, and I covered her with my parka and sweater. I held her hand while she cried. I stroked her hair when the nurse sent to draw blood had to try again and again. I do not think that in my actions there was pretense or hypocrisy. Nevertheless, as the nurses spoke to me solicitously, taking the relationship to be what it was not, I was embarrassed.

Chapter 11

The Amy who took me to stay at her apartment the night of my mother's funeral, who let me sleep in her bed with her, and who held me as I was shaking, the Amy who baked chocolate chip cookies and gave me her high school class ring, the Amy who earlier that day lit up with joy at the sight of Ed and who, while I was at Cambridge, called Jim just to see if he was all right, I was there with her. And I was with the Amy who, in the dreams from which, throughout college, I would awaken, had her hands clenched around my throat. Before she began to suffer from Alzheimer's, Amy once told me that whenever I brought friends to the house I would race up the stairs to my room. She knew, she said, I had been ashamed of her for being overweight. I remember how I tried to avoid introducing her, but that my mother had died was what I did not want to tell my junior high friends. Are times like that night in the emergency room supposed to be healing? I probed inwardly, and I could not find that I hurt any less. Waiting with her in the emergency room was almost the last time that I saw her.

The remaining years of my relationship with my father were even more difficult. Dad was moved from the house to assisted living less than a year after Amy's death, and from there he was transferred to a nursing home. Even so, the passing months were punctuated by hospital stays. Dad was on dialysis and not paying attention to his health. Fearing that he would lose his job if things continued as they were, Doug finally persuaded Dad to move to a nursing home in Ohio, and I was grateful to Doug. To bring my father to Fayetteville was not something I could have done.

One weekend I had been angry all the way from Omaha to Fayetteville. As Dad was taken to physical therapy, he had waved goodbye in a way that left me uncertain whether it mattered that I had come. Another time, as I was taking him to dinner, noticing how frail and unsteady he had become, the string that connected us seemed less tangled. "Shall I tell you something?" my father said. "When you were in college and never invited me to a football game, I thought that I had lost you. It is nice that you are here." That day I was able to reply, truthfully, that I was glad to be there. Yet weeks later I just watched as my friend Suzanne, who had accompanied me to Nebraska, coaxed my father into conversation. She cut his toenails and rubbed ointment on his arms, things I could not seem to do. Then when Doug, arriving from Ohio, said that Dad seemed happier that Doug could help him with his bedpan than he was to see his son, I was infuriated.

Psychologists tell of an experiment in which baby monkeys were given two mothers, one of wire from whom they could get food and the other without food but made of terrycloth. I did not have to be told what the infant monkeys would do. If my father had died and my mother lived, I think I would scarcely have missed him. Even as a small child I wanted always to sit on my mother's lap, never on my dad's. "Robert, say goodbye to Lynne," Amy used to insist, and deflecting embrace, Dad would turn sideways. When Bill, the priest who taught me contemplative prayer, asked me about my parents, I told him about my mother. When he asked about my father, I replied that Dad had always been remote and so had not had much effect. "That's an effect," Bill said.

Wire is a cage which, while keeping his children out, imprisoned my father. When I told Dad I had a fellowship to Cambridge, he asked if I supposed I was going to meet Socrates. Unable any longer to face his ridicule, I did not show my father my book on Aristotle when it was published. When I moved to New York, I did not tell him I was studying for ordination as a priest. Then during my first semester in seminary, at Thanksgiving, my father died.

After his death, a therapist would propose to me that my father was schizoid. That was a term I did not know, and so I looked it up in the *DSM IV*. Dad's complete inability to anticipate what it was that anyone expected of him, his sarcasm and profound negativity, the paranoia, it all fit. Time and again in our relationship, I experienced what seemed to me impenetrable obtuseness and an enormity of betrayal. Perhaps my father had been in better psychological health in his youth, before Mother's death. Certainly for him, as for me, after her death, circumstances were difficult, and no doubt he tried to do his best. Yet it seems to me that life demanded much more from my father than he had to give. My father's seems to me a life that, in some ways, never got started.

I think back to how I drove Dad around the neighborhoods near the nursing home, neighborhoods he knew from his childhood. One day he remarked, "I wish that I were satisfied." "Satisfied that . . . ?" I inquired. "Just satisfied," he said. A life that in some sense never was lived is tragic. I believe that there is more of God in my father than I experienced, but nevertheless I am uncomfortable with the question whether I loved him. In knowing my father what I knew was how he defended himself from being known.

In Christian history, that heaven is about being reunited with the people we love has not always been a prominent idea. Although St. Augustine thought of the Christian community, living and dead, as a heavenly city, in medieval thought, union with God was pre-eminent. I have seen it argued that only since the nineteenth century has reunion with family come to be what heaven is primarily about. For too many years I have longed to see my mother. I long to be together with Mopsy and Goliath, our dogs. But the absence of my father's sarcasm from my life has brought profound relief.

Chapter 12

I dreamed I was about to blast off in a rocket ship. It looked like a garbage can with a pointy top. As I crawled in, Lowell said, "When you get far into outer space, the ship and also your body will be annihilated." "What about my soul?" I asked, and Lowell replied that it should be all right. Yet he shrugged when, in my dream, he said this, as if there were some uncertainty. Lowell is now the rector of St. Paul's, but the summer of my dream he was my spiritual director. I was that summer tumbling into the deepest contemplative prayer I have ever known. And I was thinking about ordination.

It is not as if I had been considering priesthood all along. I had gone to Cambridge drawn to monastic life, and by the time I returned from Grandchamp three years later, I was expecting to settle into being a philosophy professor. But soon I was feeling restless, and so I approached Russ, St. Paul's rector at the time. I asked him about fellowships for study at an Episcopal seminary. I told Russ I was teaching a class on Platonism in late antiquity and wanted to know more about the Greek church fathers. I explained that I had lived at Grandchamp and mentioned the book I had begun to write. I added that I intended to teach an honors colloquium on Thomas Merton.

Some months before meeting with Russ, I had heard him give a homily on rules of life. In his homily he talked about a kid at church camp the previous summer who would scarcely have been noticed in New York during my seminary days, or even in Arkansas a few years later. The youngster wore black clothes and had purple hair. Russ urged his listeners to recognize and appreciate one another's strangeness. It is in our peculiarity, he said, that our giftedness can be seen. In our meeting, in answer to my question, Russ began to recount a novel he had started reading. Robertson Davies's novel was about an unusual doctor. Russ's narrative was convoluted, but its relevance was clear. I had asked Russ not about ordination but simply about seminary. Russ was asking me whether I wanted to be ordained.

Russ and I continued to meet throughout the months that followed. One night I dreamed I was driving down a slope so steep that, though I veered through brush to slow the car, I could not stop. The next night I dreamed that I was being bitten again and again by a Rattlesnake. This was no ordinary snake, but archetypal. The dream reminded me of a time in Cambridge when God had seemed so close I thought my substance, like milkweed, would disintegrate. In Cambridge, the experience recurred the following morning while I was bicycling to St. Bene't's for mass. I panicked then and asked God to go away, and to my chagrin, that is just what seemed to happen. But the summer of my strange dreams, Lowell was reassuring: "God is trustworthy, and the impending panic is only noise." Do I love God with all my heart and soul and mind and strength? Do I love God at all? Obsessed with whether God loves me, I was not sure I had ever asked that question. Then during prayer, thought and imagery ceased, and with them my sense of time's passage.

When the fall semester began, I became a lay reader and chalice bearer at St. Paul's. As a graduate student many years before, I had been the acolyte for a weekday Eucharist, but only two or three students were ever there. I feared that, in front of a congregation of several hundred, my recollectedness would dissolve in anxiety and awkwardness. Instead, love dissolved me. Those I knew, those who looked familiar, those I had never before seen—how can one say "The Blood of our Lord Jesus Christ keep you in everlasting life" and not feel God's burning tenderness? Chalice bearing spilled into my life and let me near the loneliness of someone I hardly knew. Releasing me from the suffering of self-consciousness, reading the lessons was making me a better teacher. "More than fifteen hours with nothing else to do but to gaze on you, Lord, and tell you that I love you," wrote the French mystic Charles de Foucauld. In Nazareth he would kneel before the sacrament all day long. Sunday afternoons that fall I raked the yard, but the love of God for each leaf poured through me like liquid through a sieve. I hold what I experienced to be not fantasy, but truth.

Months passed, and Russ took me to meet the bishop. The following summer my parish discernment committee began its work. There was puzzlement why I should be ordained if not to be a parish priest. There were questions about philosophy. Could a philosopher have a religious commitment that was not tentative? I remember answering a question about the university: was there a problem about the separation of church and state? And I remember a conversation about the sacraments. I told the committee I experience the sacraments from a contemplative space that is different from the discursive reason important to philosophy. I suggested that the sacraments let us experience creation as holy. I said I believe that what priesthood is essentially about, what is distinctive of it, is the priest's relation to the sacraments.

"If my parish committee turns me down, I will feel so much shame I will want to leave St. Paul's, and there is no place I want to go," I fretted at night. "I wish my friends did not know," some part of me insisted, and I replied to myself, emphatically, "That is not true." After the committee finally finished its work, Lowell and I drove to Little Rock. We were scheduled to meet the diocesan commission on ministry, a committee of laypersons and clergy.

As we were winding our way along the mountainous Ozark roads, I told Lowell I would try to be at peace whatever the outcome. Lowell replied, "I'm a sports fan, and I want to go for the win." In fact, the meeting turned out to be only the first of several, but it was, to my surprise, enjoyable. They were curious what it had been like for me to be the department chair for so many years. Questioned about what I was writing, I told them that I seemed to be able to be articulate about suffering. I was asked about practicing the presence of God, and then we talked about Merton's view of the role of silence and interior poverty in the life of a priest.

In some dioceses I am sure I would not have been ordained. My attempts to articulate what my "call" was all about were never smooth, never, even in my own eyes, very successful. The path to ordination began with an intuition, Russ's intuition, that if I could experience the sacraments as the priest does, who I am and what I write would be affected by it, and that immediately struck me as true. But how could I explain that to committees?

Meanwhile my dreams were haunted by Old Main, the historic building that houses the philosophy department. One night while I watched from just far enough away, its facade, towers and all, collapsed, falling forward on the lawn like a piece of cardboard. Another night I dreamed that I had a beautiful handmade bicycle frame. Lacking forks and head set, the bike frame was a triangle of platinum gold that was as luminous as the sun. "Regulations" required that I leave the bike frame outside Old Main, and soon it was stolen. From the window of my office, I saw the thief; his hair was long and brown, like mine except that it was curly. When I chased after him, he ran as gracefully as a god. The thief leaped high through the broken window of a gutted building on the campus and disappeared, still carrying my bicycle frame. That was how the dream ended. The thief had gone where I could not follow.

My life at the university was in fact full of frustration that academic year. I was irritated by measures intended to make colleges "accountable." I was tired of the apparent assumption that Xerox machines and computers and people never break, that productivity and efficiency and the control which brings them about can forever be increased, and that they should be. It reminded me of ironing dish towels and flannel shirts and handkerchiefs at

Grandchamp. Unrumpledness is good, but a good which did not seem to me to be the good, all things considered.

At Grandchamp the laundry was often behind, causing strain, yet no one proposed we should work faster or longer. At the university I was angry most of all at the hundreds of pages required for program evaluation by the state's department of higher education. As I documented the careers of our graduates and the undergraduate schools from which our graduate students had come, the collection of information seemed much more than excessive; it seemed an end in itself. "I sustain your life and you use it to do *this!*" thundered the heavens, or my imagination. To be department chair had been creative and good for both the department and me. But after fifteen years, I had stayed at it too long.

In *New Seeds of Contemplation* Merton wrote that to find our true selves, we must share with God in the work of creating the truth of our identity. He described the false or external self as a mask, afflicted with metaphysical poverty. He said that many poets are not poets (even if they are acclaimed) and many monks not saints just because they never get around to being the particular poet or monk God intended them to be. If God's intentions are so specific, how is it that we share with God in the creation of who we are? The answer would seem to lie in Merton's understanding of what we are intended to be. Our true selves, Merton wrote, are what all the circumstances of our individual lives call for.

I do believe that I was looking that year for a way to gather together the circumstances of my life. I think that the theft of my bicycle frame and the crashing of the facade of Old Main were about uncovering my true self. The idea of the "true self" makes sense to me, even though, just as the world is always richer than our models of it, so our understanding of one another and of ourselves is always incomplete. We sift our memories and emotions. We select and arrange according to some inner sense of how things are and what has been important, yet the result is always partial. The self that is articulated does not take into account all the circumstances of our lives, and we have not seen all the possibilities in them.

The Presocratic philosopher Heraclitus put the problem this way: "You could not discover the limits of the soul even if you traveled by every path, such is the depth of its meaning." Nevertheless, the question of what was called for by the circumstances of my life to that point took the form of asking whether I was called to be a priest. And one evening as I was feeling anxious, I seemed to be given an answer. It came in a vision, the only waking vision I have ever experienced.

In my vision, my mother and grandmother appeared and stood on either side of me. They were tall, like two archangels, and their announcement, "Lynne is *ours*, and no one is going to mess with her," was a less exalted version of the angel's words to Mary: "Fear not."

My maternal grandmother died of breast cancer when my mother was fourteen, and in my vision she looked as she did in photographs that I had seen. In their height and fierce solemnity, both my mother and grandmother resembled the archangels in a familiar icon. That the elements of my vision came from memory is obvious, but all our experience, including experience of God, has to be mediated by what is within us. How else could it be? Yet I accepted that vision as an answer. It had addressed my deepest fears.

Chapter 13

Rita and I built a spaceship in my backyard. We made it out of a cardboard box big enough for us to eat and sleep in. Before that box became our spaceship, it had been the container for my parents' new refrigerator. Dressed in our knit pajamas, we armed ourselves with waterguns. As we traveled to the moon and several planets, our communication link to Earth was the spray attachment from the kitchen sink. "The moon shines east. The moon shines west. It is made of green cheese with rat holes in it. The weather on the moon is fine when the weather on the moon is fine," we wrote in our log. On the third day (adult time) just as we were approaching Jupiter, Rita's mother insisted on taking her shopping, and that ended our adventure.

Rita and I had been best friends ever since my mother lifted me over the fence between our yards when I was three and she was five. Camped out one night in Rita's backyard, we pricked our fingers and rubbed them together, making us blood sisters. Then we buried a time capsule filled with plastic jumping beans in her mother's garden to commemorate the event. One summer we tried to string a tin can telephone between our bedroom windows, but the line got tangled in the trees. Another summer, Rita and her younger sister Maureen and I staged a circus, performing acrobatics on the swing set. The three of us started a long-lasting club, the SSJCC. The mission of the Secret Society Junk Collecting Club was to hunt for bric-a-brac and broken tools in the neighborhood's alleys. We sold the junk to our mothers and stored our earnings in a metal band-aid box. We would buy a Hardy Boys book whenever we had saved a hundred pennies.

Some years ago I visited Rita in California, and we went camping near the ocean. I saw Kristi, my college apartmentmate, on that same trip out West. And I have stayed in touch, mostly by phone, ever since graduate school with Renee, who lives in Michigan. Yet when Elizabeth, a history professor and a member of St. Paul's, asked me to lunch, I was too preoccupied with the philosophy department to want new women friends. Nevertheless, somehow, a few years later, it was Elizabeth who gave a dinner party to celebrate the publication of my book on Aristotle and my promotion.

As six of us, all women, sat in Elizabeth's greenhouse after dinner, watching the rain, I told my new friends that the party had been sacred. From graduate school twenty-five years earlier to my new rank was continuation, but that the occasion had been shared with women from St. Paul's was astounding grace, all-out surprise. For me it was less a celebration of my promotion from associate professor to professor than of women's friendships. The depression I had experienced following surgery two years before taught me how much I needed friends. It also began to matter to me that more of my friends be women.

As a philosopher and a priest, I have male friends, more than many women do. Moreover, the differences between the lives of women who do not have children and those who do, especially when their children are young, can feel unbridgeable. On the other hand, friendships that were professional, at least in their origin, became less satisfying to me at midlife. I was weary of competitiveness, even though I am not free of it myself. The task oriented character of work relationships seemed an implicit assertion that things in our lives were fine. As department chair, I knew my colleagues well enough to know that was not always true, yet what had come to feel like pretense intensified my sense of isolation. Having friends outside the philosophy department made it less problematic for me to be vulnerable. And I had learned that women tend to hug more freely.

Then the summer before I left for seminary, all my friends from St. Paul's, women and men, clergy and lay, really were friends to me. When my gynecologist told me he could not be completely sure the mass on my remaining ovary was endometriosis, it was not news I was expecting. But only days later Ann and Suzanne were in the hospital waiting room. This time the surgery was done in Fayetteville, and they were there along with Jim. We held hands and prayed together, an event Jim dubbed the "pregame huddle," and after that, Jim and I kissed goodbye.

Four years earlier, a nurse's spooning ice into my mouth was what recalled me to consciousness. This time, until Jim told me the endometriosis was much worse than even the surgeon expected, I did not remember anything at all. When next I awoke, Suzanne was waiting in a rocking chair. My sleep seemed less hallucinatory than the first time I had surgery and less broken.

The following morning it was raining when the doctor came by. Someone from maintenance was banging wastebaskets as the nurses conferred about the electrical risk from a puddle. Every movement and sound making me more nauseous, I whispered a futile request that they do their talking in the hall. Yet by afternoon, when my St. Paul's friends arrived, I wanted everyone, even if quietly and one at a time, to come in. I was so grateful to them for their presence. It was gratitude that flowed through me in waves, a gratitude that in its intensity I have rarely felt.

Just before surgery, alone on a cart in the hospital hall, I had become aware of God—or perhaps my mother. It was a gravitational force so great as to be irresistible. No other attraction, neither Jim and friends, nor ordination, nor unfinished writing, could withstand love that intense. Even though I had asked the people of St. Paul's to pray for my health, I was in that hallway suddenly so unsure what I wanted that I began to cry. Twenty-four hours later I was grateful to be alive. Nonetheless the approach of death is nothing to be feared if death brings love like that.

Jim was able to stay home through the weeks that followed, and I had so many friends in Fayetteville. It had been major abdominal surgery once again, but I was sure recovery would be very different. I believed that Jim and friendships and my excitement about seminary would carry me through. I thought of surgery the second time as a chance to relive an experience and get it right. Yet in four years I had forgotten what it is like to be too weak to spit out toothpaste. After I left the hospital, a truck backed down the hill in front of our house much too fast, barely missing me, and I could not jump aside. Sleeping and waking came so abruptly those first weeks that it was only the clock which told me I had slept. Then, a month after surgery, just as abruptly, I could not sleep at all.

Some nights Jim stayed awake to keep me company, and we watched the sunrise. When my doctor said I could resume normal exercise, not having slept, I went running one morning at 5 a.m. But more often at night any activity, even reading, seemed too much effort. I avoided caffeine. I drank warm milk before bed. I considered calling my doctor, but in my few experiences with sleeping pills, I have found that they leave me more sleepless than I was before. I practiced contemplative prayer, and I prayed for sleep. Even so, my inability to sleep lasted so long that I started to wonder if sleep would ever come. I was, despite everything, on the edge of depression. Then, sleep returned, just as abruptly as it had stopped, and with it, my spirits lifted.

As I packed for New York, Jim and I began to realize that we had been apart for seven years. We asked ourselves why we continued making the choices we did. But Jim still wanted to return to Illinois, and I was well along in the ordination process. Because I had studied philosophy, seminary would take only three semesters and one summer, and there would be long vacations. Besides, we were sure Jim would have to make frequent trips to New York to take care of his mother. In fact, Jim and I would be separated four more years although we did not know that then. As I was packing for seminary, our ambivalence was already so great that we made no attempt to rent out the house. By the time we finally admitted the house would be empty, it was mid-August. We just gave the key to Alison, another of my friends from St. Paul's, and asked her to look in.

The week I moved from Fayetteville, there were farewell parties. The guidebooks to Manhattan I was given came back to Arkansas well-worn. Cindy and Suzanne sprayed an old pair of sandals, my habitual footwear, with red glitter. Like Dorothy who was given red shoes to protect her on her way to see the wizard who would send her homeward, my friends wanted me to remember to come home.

Yet job changes and remarriage and health concerns took Cindy and Lynn and Alison and Elizabeth to California and Colorado and Mississippi. While I was in seminary or soon afterward, many of my closest women friends would move away. Somehow I had assumed that, in making friends at midlife with women in Arkansas, we would be together for the rest of our lives. But it was not so.

As we parted, we vowed to stay in touch by email and phone and to visit one another, and that mostly has not happened. As we parted, I thought I would acknowledge their importance in my life by making new friends, and that has not been as easy as I supposed. Jim's return, renewed interest in philosophy, and my changed role at St. Paul's have often pushed friendships into the background. Even decisions Jim and I made, thinking they would encourage us to be more social, have just as often had the opposite effect.

We live in time and can attend to only one thing, or at most a few things, at a time. Our lives, however full, are almost always out of balance, and there is inevitably something that is at least as important as what we are doing that is being ignored. That seems not to be a condition we can overcome by trying harder, which is not to say we should not try, but only that we can know in advance we will fail. "What has been done has been done; what has not been done has not been done. Let it be." This is from the service for night prayer in *A Prayer Book for New Zealand*. It is by tacking that sailboats move into the wind.

Chapter 14

General Seminary is in Chelsea, near the Hudson River just north of Greenwich Village. The grounds were donated by Clement Clark Moore, who wrote "The Night before Christmas." The gardens provide a haven from the concrete of New York City, and the old brick buildings are on the historic register. Most students and faculty live on the close (the seminary grounds), as did I. At General, I had both faculty and student friends.

From Chelsea, I explored Manhattan on foot past the World Trade Center south to Battery Park and east to South Street Seaport. I walked north through Central Park to Columbia and the Cathedral of St. John the Divine. I discovered how to buy discounted theater tickets, and I visited the museums many times. But more than anything else, it was seminary that I found exciting. The program I was in had been designed primarily for clergy in other traditions who were becoming Episcopal priests, and so it was flexible. I enrolled in courses not only at General but at Union, the venerable Protestant seminary on the Upper West Side where Tillich and Niebuhr once taught. I took very few classes for credit because I wanted to audit as many as I could. Every Friday evening I would begin the reading for the following week. Throughout the weekend I read and read and read.

I arrived at seminary interested in Christian thought in late antiquity. Richard Norris, who knew as much about the early centuries as any scholar anywhere, was officially retired, but another student and I asked him to do a readings course on Origen. Origen, who lived in the third century, wrote highly influential allegorical interpretations of scripture. When scripture is read allegorically, what is said is taken to convey another meaning. Allegorical readings were ubiquitous in late antiquity. Greek writers read Homer as a journey of the soul, and in Galatians Paul interpreted the story of Abraham's two wives, Hagar and Sarah, as about the old and new covenants. When Isaac restores the wells the Philistines had filled with earth, Origen suggested, the Philistines are those who lose the spiritual meaning of the Law. Isaac is said to be drawing out the living water in the soul. Origen claimed that we will find God within if we throw out the earth of carnal feelings.

Did the author of Genesis really intend that the story be read as Origen read it? On the other hand, if the meaning of a text is to be found in the response of its readers, does it even make sense to ask if an interpretation is correct? On Origen's theory of the biblical text, the author of scripture is Christ the Logos, and so the answer to both these questions can be "yes." The purpose of reading scripture is for us to encounter the God who is hidden. Because scripture addresses souls of all conditions, many different meanings can be right. Scripture teaches morality, and, for Origen, it teaches doctrine, which means that it teaches who Jesus is. In reading scripture, we are like dogs on a trail who sometimes lose the scent but can find it again, wrote Origen. We are able to find it because the inner self is a true image of God. If we persevere in reading scripture, Origen believed, even when the text remains obscure, Christ becomes present in us.

Allegorical readings of scripture enabled the early church (as well as the Jewish philosopher Philo) to uphold the sacred authorship of the text despite problematic passages. The stories of violence and treachery in Hebrew scripture could be accounted for. Their apparent subjects were not what such stories were really about. Like all Platonists in late antiquity, Origen was focused on eternal truths. He saw poetry and history and narrative detail as unworthy of the word of God. Reading allegorically offered an explanation for the presence of these in scripture. Poetry and history were the marks of riddles.

The tradition of reading scripture allegorically continued until the rise of modern science. From the seventeenth century on, as nature ceased to be "read" symbolically, as in alchemy, for example, so scripture ceased to be read symbolically too. Curiously, the very thing that bored Origen, namely, the historical, is what interests us most. The difficulty of determining what in the Bible is historical often frustrates modern readers.

For seminarians, the historical critical study of scripture can be unsettling, but I found the disputes familiar. "What do we know about the historical Jesus?" presents problems very similar to those raised by a question I had already thought about: "What do we know about the historical Socrates?" Like Jesus, Socrates was condemned to death by the state for his teachings. Like Jesus, Socrates wrote nothing yet inspired a body of literature from which we try to reconstruct who he was and what he taught. Like the Gospels, the portraits of Socrates we have from Plato and Xenophon and Aristophanes are very different.

Gregory Vlastos, the great Platonic scholar of the mid-twentieth century, thought he could distinguish the views of the historical Socrates from those that were Plato's own, even if in many of Plato's dialogues the latter were presented by "Socrates." Everyone agrees that Socrates tried to provoke thought by convincing Athenians they did not know what virtue is, but Vlastos argued that Socrates would talk philosophy on street corners with anyone while Plato wanted students already to know mathematics. Socrates limited himself to ethics, Vlastos thought, but Plato was interested also in metaphysics and epistemology. Socrates claimed he did not know what death is (yet trusting the gods, he was willing to die rather than abandon philosophy). Plato, on the other hand, offered four proofs for the immortality of the soul.

Vlastos's work produced a near consensus when I was in graduate school. However, a younger generation of scholars has begun to question the circularity of his arguments. Vlastos thought we learn most about the historical Socrates from the dialogues earliest in Plato's career, but his hypotheses about which dialogues were early too often were based on their "Socratic" content. Most scholars now refer to "Plato's Socrates," in other words, Socrates as we know him through Plato's text. Many are reluctant to make substantial inferences about the historical Socrates at all. Living with uncertainty about Socrates prepared me for the study of the Gospels. Jesus is both illumined and obscured by the texts through which we know him.

At seminary I learned to see the Gospel stories as shaped by their place in a literary whole. Jesus' "Sermon on the Mount" is on the Mount because the author of Matthew conceptualized Jesus as the new Moses (in Luke a similar collection of sayings is given on a plain). The Ascension seems to be modeled on Elijah's ascent. To see the stories as telling us how the early church interpreted Jesus through the persons and events in Hebrew scripture made a lot of sense to me. Encountering the Gospels as literary texts enriched their meaning even though to read them in this way is to concede how little about the historical Jesus we actually know. Before seminary was over, I did suffer doubt and confusion about God on account of scripture, but the cause was not historical scholarship; it was feminist thought. What began to disturb me was scripture's misogyny.

My adviser told me I should be sure to take Phyllis Trible's course at Union, Women Writing on the Bible. I had not read her books, *God and the Rhetoric of Sexuality* or *Texts of Terror*, but I quickly came to realize what influence Trible has had. All semester we read familiar passages whose words I had never really heard, and we read passages of scripture I did not even know were there. By the second week I understood why the Bible has left many women I know angry and hurt. By the third week I was angry.

When the Israelites worship other gods, Hosea describes this as Israel's "whoring." "I will strip her naked and expose her as in the day she was born, and make her like a wilderness, and turn her into a parched land, and kill her with thirst" is what the prophet has God say. Water and clothing are withheld from Israel, depicted as female. Then God humiliates Israel by exposing her genitalia before her lovers and allows no one to rescue her. In the end, God speaks tenderly and seductively to Israel, like an abusive lover.

Reading such passages, I lost the detachment that would have let me appreciate the prophet's skill with metaphor. Instead, I was mad at the ancient Israelites, and men generally, and by the term's conclusion, I was mad at God. When I told this to my bishop, he replied that now I would understand what so many women feel and for that he was glad. I will never again be able to read Hosea or Jeremiah or Ezekiel without noticing what the words really say. Yet the lasting influence of Trible's course has not for me been anger. Instead I began to question what it means for a text to be sacred.

At my ordination I would be asked if I believed that scripture, which in that context clearly meant Hebrew and Christian scripture, contains all things necessary to salvation. I replied, truthfully, that I do. Nevertheless, without denying that scripture is in some sense sacred, I have become convinced just how thoroughly a human product scripture is. In the Bible we find a people's understanding of God, one that sometimes does and sometimes does not transcend the assumptions of the cultures in which it was written. This is as true of scripture as it is of Plato or Shakespeare or any other texts that we revere. In the sixteenth century, Anglicanism's foundational theologian Richard Hooker described the sources of our knowledge of God as grounded in "natural law." He held that just as we evaluate reason and tradition by scripture, so we must also evaluate scripture by what we know through reason and from tradition.

Chapter 15

I called Ann Ulanov to ask permission to audit her class even though I had taken none of the prerequisites. She suggested I come the first night and see if it was the right knowledge at the right time in my life. When Bill taught me to pray, he lent me Ann's book about our unconscious images of God. Something in *Picturing God* made me want to keep reading even as I found the language of depth psychology perplexing. I bought and read as many of her books as I could find. Years later, after moving to New York, I looked at the back cover of one of her books and saw something I had forgotten. A supervising analyst on the faculty of the Jung Institute in New York, Ann Ulanov was (and is) a distinguished professor of psychiatry and religion at Union.

In her course that spring, I read Freud and Melanie Klein and D.W. Winnicott, among many others. Winnicott was an English pediatrician, influenced by Freud and Klein, who wrote about how human beings grow from infancy into becoming themselves. In the language of psychoanalysis, an infant's ruthless feeding is described as destruction. By accepting her infant's aggressiveness, Winnicott said, a good enough mother lets the infant see that its destructiveness can be survived.

Thus it is from the mother's constancy that an infant learns to trust the world and to trust itself. On the other hand, if the world were always perfectly adapted to the child's every need, mothers and infants would remain merged in what Winnicott called the mother-infant dyad. Never to discover that the mother is a separate person would be not to know that the world is "outside." Since a child cannot become a self without an awareness of what is "other," parental failures are necessary for the child's development. So being intruded upon, or sometimes deprived, can be catastrophic, or it can be beneficial. Which it is depends on its scope and timing.

Chapter 15

The semester of Ann's course, I was also auditing a course in pastoral counseling at General Seminary. The topic for the last class was bereavement that goes unrecognized, and I suggested the grief of children. What I said fit easily into the conversation, but the instructor must have sensed I was speaking from experience. At the break she asked me, "Are you OK?" and I replied, "Yes." When class was over, I went to evensong.

The faculty processed into the chapel in their academic hoods. David Hurd is an incomparable organist who improvises with marvelous creativity. I always looked forward to hearing him play. But that night, amid all the pageantry, as the seminary community chanted the Psalms, I was surrounded by an abyss. It was a void into which I had been swallowed, a darkness in which I felt all but extinguished. To be in that abyss was frightening, yet familiar. It seemed to be something long forgotten. I knew that my adolescence had been haunted by that sense of simultaneous being and nonbeing.

I could not shake off the experience of that night. The next morning in the midst of all the formality of worship in General's chapel, as we sang "Thy strong word did cleave the darkness . . .," I began to cry. Wanting to talk to someone far away from the seminary community, I called a Presbyterian minister of an Upper East Side church whom I happened to know, and it turned out that he had been a classmate of Ann's. I told him that I thought the intensity of her course that semester had caused what was unconscious to surface. He was sure that she would want to know.

In seminary I had more self-confidence than in all my previous years in school. In my other courses, I spoke up readily. Even though I read voraciously and kept resolving to participate, in Ann's course I was tongue-tied. Maybe in class most of my energy was unavailable to consciousness; I could not know. I do know that I was awed by Ann. The extremity of my shyness made doing what the minister urged difficult, but I had to do something. Somehow I managed to approach her at the end of the last class.

I felt so clumsy standing there, juggling my backpack and raincoat and umbrella. We walked down the stairs together, and I tried to explain. Ann said I felt all but obliterated because my ego had been nearly obliterated. "When someone close to us dies, a piece of us dies," she said, and that piece had been nearly the whole. Ann told me that the double awareness I described was breakdown. I can feel panic over things as trivial as misspelling a word. "That is fear of a breakdown," Ann said. She suggested that I read Winnicott's "Fear of Breakdown." Long before the Vietnam War made "posttraumatic stress" a part of ordinary speech, Winnicott proposed that fear can be fear of a breakdown that has already happened.

Winnicott wrote that if an infant has to wait too long for its mother to return, the infant cannot keep its belief in her existence alive in its mind. The experience is traumatic and incomprehensible. As a primitive agony that has no conceptual place, it destroys the infant's sense of a continuous self. The effect of this experience that cannot be integrated is recurrent panic, and the panic appears to be an exaggerated fear of disintegration in the event of future loss. In reality, however, the anticipated future is not so much the object of the fear as an occasion for remembering. The panic is an unconscious remembrance of actual past disintegration.

I read "Fear of Breakdown" over and over. Even when I was unsure what he was saying, reading Winnicott I felt safe and understood. I identified with the infant that he described. That may seem odd since I was long past infancy when my mother died. I was twelve. But the death of a parent is much more than an overlong absence. It is a disappearance that lasts the rest of one's life. The permanence of death is what makes it so incomprehensible.

The death of my mother was the death of the person on whom I depended to interpret my experiences for me. How could I integrate my mother's death into my experience when it was my mother who made me understandable to myself? Before starting seminary, I had supposed that I was done with therapy. After all, I had recovered from depression and gone through the ordination process. Yet after that conversation, even before I left New York, I called Sabra Hassel, who, until her retirement, was Fayetteville's most respected clinical psychologist. After her doctorate, Sabra had studied in the summers at the Masterson Institute in New York. We talked several times while I was home, and then, reluctantly, I returned to New York for the summer. There was no accredited CPE in northwest Arkansas, and I had to do CPE.

Clinical Pastoral Education is part of the preparation for ordination in many denominations. The eleven week summer program I was in consisted of five days and one overnight at the hospital each week and two weekends of staying there on call. At 7:30 every morning I would leave for Penn Station, a twenty minute walk from the seminary. Even if the trains were on time, it would be 7 p.m. when I got back. Most evenings there was also reading to be done or preparation for leading worship, and there were analyses of conversations with patients to be written.

The seminarians the previous summer had been furious about CPE, and no doubt their stories triggered my fears. But once I entered the hospital, my experience was all my own. On the first day, after a tour of the hospital, we were asked where we would like to work. I had a strong desire to avoid the cancer ward and an interest in psychiatry, which could not be satisfied by the program I was in. Apart from that, I had neither interests nor preferences. The hospital seemed to me a prison, a place without sky, or sun.

I wanted to be home in Arkansas where I could talk to Sabra about the debris of the ancient breakdown I had uncovered. I wanted to be still and turn inward and try to ponder the evident truth that had so shaken my assumptions about myself. I wanted to write, and I wanted to be with Jim.

Instead, night after night I was returning to the seminary exhausted, in need of time for exercise and prayer, and yet with preparation for the next day still to be done. On Saturday morning, if the week was finally over, I would load a washing machine in the community's laundry. Then I would go back to my room and sleep. But after two weeks, the weekends were not long enough to be reparative. For the rest of the summer, all the time, I was almost crying.

"Don't you have meetings where you process this stuff?" my seminarian friend Barbara asked me one evening as I was complaining. In fact, there were group meetings and the members of my group were good people, and I had meetings with our supervisor, a caring person who tried to help. Yet whatever happened in those meetings did not resolve anything. They just added to the tumult. Because I had been chair of a philosophy department, everyone assumed I would be a leader, and by being so withdrawn, in an unfortunate way I was. Instead of the spontaneous conversation that was supposed to occur in our meetings, our group would sometimes just sit in silence. Communal silence can be restful and reassuring, but this silence was not like that at all.

Hospital chaplains need to be able to establish rapport quickly with a long and ever-changing roster of patients. Before I could bring myself to enter any patient's room, I would circle the ward three or four times. I walked the seven flights of stairs instead of taking the elevator in order to use up time and be alone. I never knew most of the patients, and I did not get to know the staff. Lowell, newly installed as rector of St. Paul's, stayed in contact almost daily by email or phone. Despite my discouragement, Lowell would not allow me to doubt that I was called to be a priest. He was a steady source of sympathy and humor and advice. Yet the question I needed most to be asked did not come from him or any professional.

Jim was in Brooklyn part of that summer, and the rest of the time he was in Fayetteville. We talked on the phone every night. "Well, Alice," he said one evening, calling me by my first name as he always does. "You never wanted to be a hospital chaplain, and it turns out that you are not ideally suited for it, right?" When I agreed, he asked the question I could not answer: "So what's the problem?"

Chapter 16

I remember the Black man, a drug user with HIV, who cried because his hair had lost its curl and then felt shame that he had cried. And I remember an old man on dialysis whose children did not visit him. There was a blind man who reminded me of my dad; we prayed the Lord's Prayer as he held my hand. When we had finished, he started to recite the 23rd Psalm, but he could not remember what came after "He leadeth me beside still waters" and I could not remember either. And once when I went to his room, his call bell had been left out of reach, which made me mad.

I met Catholics who were angry at their church for being too conservative and Episcopalians who were angry with theirs for being too liberal. With the exception of African American congregations, the very old of almost every religious tradition told me that, once they were no longer able to go to church, the church ceased to be interested in them. A young man was so discouraged about his illness that he said whenever he would visit the shark tanks at the aquarium, he wanted to jump in. And there was the woman whose beautiful young granddaughter had died in a car accident some years before. She was grieving, and I could not think of anything I could say.

Nights on call in the hospital were eerie. One night I was awakened when a relative of a patient told me his dying brother wanted to confess to a Catholic priest. The dying man was in so much pain that I was frightened, but I should have tried harder to figure out what he really wanted. Instead I complied and found a telephone.

The next morning the man who had asked me to call a priest happened to see me in the coffee shop. "I know God arranged for me to be at my brother's side so that I could force him to make his confession," he said. "I am the only one in the family who could do it, and it is what I was put on this earth to do!" Feeling outraged and dismayed at the part I had played, I called Lowell, who tried to reassure me that the rituals of dying are for the living. I spoke to my supervisor, who said, "Today is another day, and so forget it." Yet theirs was advice I was not able to follow. Dying seems to me holy space that should not be violated.

I remember a man I had been visiting at the request of the nurses. He had a reputation for being difficult, but I found him to be gentle. When he died alone in the night, although I suppose my distress reflected my need more than his, I was upset that the nurses forgot to call. It baffled my supervisor that I could desire so desperately not to be in CPE and still care about the patients that I came to know. But I could never see the contradiction. I did not want to be at the hospital, but I was there and so were they. In a hospital the chaplain is the only staff member with discretionary time, and even though I found it hard to start conversations, years of contemplative prayer had made me attentive. I would gladly listen, and to listen was to care.

All summer long I carried in my pocket the phone number of a clinical psychologist Sabra knew in New York. The seminary's professor of pastoral theology, aware that I was depressed, urged me to call her, but I never made the call. To phone someone I did not know would have taken more energy than I had, and I worried that I would miss appointments whenever the trains were late. But my real fear was that a therapist would tell me to quit CPE. And even if she did not, I was afraid that if I began to reflect on what I was experiencing, I would be unable to finish the program. I had to complete CPE in order to be ordained.

In *Memories, Dreams, Reflections,* Jung says that, during World War I, military psychiatrists would pull a man from the front lines if he began to dream nothing but war scenes. Unceasing dreams of the war were thought to show that the soldier no longer possessed any psychic defenses. How much psychiatrists at the time of the First World War understood about the human mind I do not know, but reading Jung, I thought of CPE. Hard though I found it to sleep that summer, when I slept, I never rested. I never seemed to reach a state of deep and dreamless sleep. Every night, if I slept, I would dream of the hospital. Sleep just duplicated the events of the day. It was the psychological equivalent of having one's eyelids pinned open.

It seemed there was not enough time, even at night, for me to make my experiences mine. It was as if my mind was too saturated to have room for dreams that might symbolize or comment on the day's events. All my dreams were repetition. Moreover, with my unconscious no longer able to be creative, even my dreams were no longer my own. I would have readily agreed that I was miserable, but with my mind so dominated, was there really still an "I"? It seemed that I was losing my sense of myself.

At the end of the last day but one, I ran up the subway stairs and out on Seventh Avenue all but shouting for joy. On the last day I went straight from the hospital to the airport. I needed to be in Arkansas for a meeting with the diocesan commission on ministry. I told everyone a few stories from CPE, and I told them that I needed rest. They could see for themselves that I was tired. To my relief, they did not press me very hard.

CPE did not end even when it was over, however. Memories of the hospital continued their grip on my dreams. My classes that fall, including another with Ann, ought to have been exciting, but I was not finding them so. It was my last semester and I was determined to enjoy seminary, but I could not seem to find my way back to the things that once had mattered. Near the end of October, I finally resolved to call the psychologist whose Manhattan phone number was still folded in my wallet. Then I called Jim instead and said I was going to the theater.

I had seen *CATS* three times since arriving in New York. First I had gone alone, and again when my ten year old nephew Arthur was visiting. The third time it was with Jim. The lighting and cat costumes and the junkyard on the stage I found magical time after time. The music and the dancing and T.S. Eliot's poetry delighted me, and the talent of the actors left me in awe. Jim and I had also seen *Phantom of the Opera* and *Les Misérables* during the summer. But that fall I ventured beyond the Broadway hits.

I bought a ticket at the TKTS half price booth to see a modern production of *Romeo and Juliet* with an all male cast. In *Shakespeare's R&J*, Juliet was innocent and vulnerable. The staging was minimal, and four actors took all the parts. A few days later, I watched Zoë Wanamaker play Electra with a nearly unbearable intensity. I went to one-person shows, shows imported from England for short runs in New York, and shows that failed. Many years ago, Rita and I used to go into the attic of my house and practice crowing like Peter Pan. Just before Christmas, in a theater filled mostly with children, I heard Peter Pan crow.

The theater created imaginary worlds that drew me out of the world within my mind. It freed my thoughts from their imprisonment and breathed enough life into my spirit that I could enjoy my last weeks in New York. Jim was taking care of his mother in Brooklyn most of that fall. I finished my classes and preached in the seminary chapel and did my practice Eucharist. I was sorry to leave, but also happy to be moving home, as I said goodbye to friends.

My first semester in seminary, Jim and I had thought that driving home for Christmas would be romantic, and that holiday it was. By "home" we meant our house in Arkansas, where in recent years we had so rarely been together. The look of the Missouri hills was wonderfully familiar. Driving through the Ozarks, we sang Christmas carols and reminisced about every town we passed. On a dark night we crunched through oak leaves a foot deep on the way to our front door. The house was empty and undisturbed, and we fell asleep together in our own bed. But a year later, when I had finished seminary, the drive to Arkansas was nothing like that.

The boiler at the seminary had broken, and the heat had been off in my rooms for a week. Jim arrived early, and although I had already carried nearly everything down from my fourth floor rooms, it was 2 p.m. when we finished loading the truck. We crossed into Pennsylvania that afternoon, and Jim noticed how low the rental truck was riding. At the rental office I had been asked how much furniture I had, and it did not occur to me to mention the books. I thought that Jim was being foolish when he insisted that we find a U-Haul dealer and exchange vehicles, but he was adamant, and so we did. Long before we reached Arkansas, I knew he had been right.

The next night, in the middle of Pennsylvania, the lock on the truck froze in the bitter cold. On our third day on icy roads, we reached Ohio but did not get as far as my brother's house, where we intended to sleep. By then Jim was wishing that I had just shipped everything and flown home from New York. I had ordination exams to prepare for, but the extra days of travel were using up my study time and I was irritable. Then when we finally arrived at his apartment in Illinois on New Year's Eve, so did a blizzard.

By the second day of January, two feet of drifting snow had blanketed the roads. The wind was so bitter that I could scarcely breathe as I walked a few blocks to a convenience store and bought whatever was still on the shelves. Meanwhile, Jim's mother had fallen. She was unhurt, but frightened, and she wanted Jim to return to Brooklyn immediately. In fact, that was impossible. The local airport was closed.

On January 4th, the day my ordination exams were scheduled to begin, we were still snowbound in Illinois. The temperature was sixteen below zero and the winds ferocious as we cleared away enough snow to free the truck. The next morning as we crept out to the interstate, passing trucks sprayed the windshield with snow, and we found that the wiper fluid was frozen. By evening we had not yet made it to St. Louis, usually a four hour drive. When we finally arrived in Fayetteville, it was eleven days after leaving New York.

Jim flew back to New York City from Fayetteville, and he arrived to find his mother weaker. Over the phone he explained to me that he might have to be there until she died, something he imagined would happen within a couple of months. I was unhappy that he was in Brooklyn, but I was glad to be in Arkansas, where I took my ordination exams even as the university's semester was beginning. And with seminary completed, I could look forward to ordination. I would be ordained a deacon in April and to the priesthood the following December.

Chapter 17

It took a lot of phone calls to find a Saturday when Bishop Maze and Mitties and Lowell were free. Mitties DeChamplain is General Seminary's professor of homiletics. She had become a good friend, and I wanted her to preach. We began by looking at January. When my ordination as a deacon was finally set for April 24th, it seemed very far away. Then the semester started.

I was teaching three classes, and I started therapy to try to understand my experience in CPE, just as I had promised myself that I would. The house had been so neglected through the years we were away that there were raccoons inhabiting the crawl space. But restoring order seemed to answer to some inner imperative. That winter I cleaned every closet, throwing out a decade of accumulated clutter. I raked the yard and filled a hundred lawn and leaf bags with wet, decaying leaves. I made the long winter drive to Nebraska to visit my brother Ed. During spring break, because Jim was in Brooklyn, I returned to New York City. I finished my last paper for seminary while I was there. At St. Paul's, the congregation prayed in the Sunday liturgy for "Lynne, who is preparing for ordination." The semester, so full of endings and beginnings, in some strange way was, I think, preparation for ordination.

Diaconal ministry is about serving the poor, the weak, the sick, and the lonely, states the Book of Common Prayer. Out of respect for those whose real call is the diaconate, the Episcopal Church may soon end the practice of first ordaining priests as deacons. I tried to persuade myself that students are vulnerable, and some of them are poor and many lonely. In fact, being a "transitional" deacon for eight months proved very helpful at least to me. To experience the ordination service twice made me more mindful of what was happening. To be clergy but not yet a priest gave me time to accustom myself to my new condition. Friends ordained at midlife warned me that relationships within the church often change: "Suddenly you are assumed to be impossibly pastoral and wise." For myself, I noticed more the encounters with strangers.

Though I seldom wear clericals except on Sunday mornings, sometimes I would stop for groceries on my way home from St. Paul's. It took time for me to get used to the reactions clerical clothing can bring. Usually people are friendly, and sometimes deferential, to a degree which still startles me. Occasionally someone is hostile, either overtly or by making a joke. Often people are puzzled and curious: "Are you a priest?" In New York no one would have noticed, but in Fayetteville, at least when worn by a woman, clericals are hard to ignore.

Jim was in Brooklyn all that winter and spring. As soon as the semester came to an end, I sublet rooms for the summer on the seminary grounds. When I returned to Fayetteville, the fall semester disappeared much too quickly. Besides teaching and being in therapy, I was taking voice lessons; I needed to learn to chant. In early December I made a brief preordination retreat at a nearby Benedictine convent, and on December 11, 1999, I was ordained a priest.

The day before my ordination, Jim arrived from New York, as did Mitties. My brother Doug brought his family with him from Ohio, and several friends drove to Fayetteville from central Arkansas and Mississippi. There were roles in the liturgy for friends as readers and presenters. At the rehearsal I suddenly realized that never since childhood birthday parties, not even at our wedding, had I seen so many of the people I love gathered in one place.

Jim grew up Catholic but no longer thinks of himself as religious, and over breakfast he asked me about communion. We were married in the Episcopal Church, and before Jim decided to receive communion then, he and the priest had a conversation about what is meant by the word "God" that went on so long I began to wonder if the wedding would take place. Wary, I told him that for Anglicans meaning emerges from participation, and whatever he did was fine. He did choose to receive, perhaps to avoid social awkwardness. Had the circumstances been reversed, I think I would have done the same.

After the service, the choirmaster said they did not sing their best, but that is not how I remember it. The Bishop chanted the "Veni Creator Spiritus," and with a weight both physical and metaphysical, all the priests who were present laid their hands on me. I was vested in a linen chasuble that was a gift from Lowell, a poncho of the kind worn by Anglican clergy in Peru. My Uncle Bob is a retired Lutheran pastor and my Aunt Joyce a liturgical weaver. They had come from Minnesota for the service, and they presented me with a beautiful set of woolen stoles. I felt honored that family and friends, several of my colleagues and even students, as well as so many parishioners, would come to my ordination. My colleague Jacob was studying to be a rabbi, and at the reception afterward he blessed me.

While I was still in seminary, I had read *The Priest's Handbook*, and I studied the rubrics in the Book of Common Prayer. In my seminary rooms I practiced making the sign of the cross over the people in front of the mirror above the bathroom sink. As I practiced, I found that I did not know when or how to place the bread on the paten and pour the wine and water into the chalice. Despite all the Eucharists I had seen, I could not remember when to fold my hands and when to raise my arms in the orans position. Yet even in my practice Eucharist at the seminary, my confusion and anxiety did not dampen my joy. I knew the consecration was not valid; I had not been ordained. But to me even my practice Eucharist felt sacred.

At my ordination, I concelebrated the Eucharist with the Bishop. I said to the congregation, "The Peace of the Lord be always with you," and, as the service ended, I offered the blessing. The following morning I presided at all three services at St. Paul's, each of them different. Sunday was nothing like concelebrating with the Bishop. That morning I discovered how daunting it can be to preside alone.

When the weekend was over, I lay awake at night too excited to sleep, wondering what it was that had happened. Traditionally, ordination has been thought of as an "ontological change," and Mitties said in her sermon, "Lynne, you are being reborn a priest." In *The Sign of Jonas*, Merton's first entry after his ordination is May 29, 1949, three days after the event: "I could not begin to write about the ordination, about saying Mass, about the *Agape* that lasted three days, with all those who came down to attend. Perhaps some day it will come out retrospectively, in fragments." Much better writers than I have been rendered inarticulate by the experience of ordination. In fact, Merton goes on, as I have, to write mostly about who was there.

To write about who was there, and how I was dressed, and what was sung may seem superficial, like the coverage of a wedding on the society page. In fact, it seems to me that writing about the occasion is a way of approaching the sacramental. Of course, we can ask more abstractly, "what is an ordination?" or "what is a marriage?" but theology often falls short of what we know through feeling. Ceremony is how reverence is expressed communally, and whatever I know of priesthood has emerged with the passage of time and from experience.

For at least a month after my ordination, I had a sense of peace, which, whenever I am presiding at the Eucharist, returns even now. It is hard to find words to describe the awe and tenderness I feel at the altar. In the Eucharist I am aware of that mysterious solidarity that enfolds us all into the One. And in my first Eucharist, I found to my surprise that I was much less nervous than I expected to be and less self-conscious, even about chanting.

To preside at the Eucharist is to offer prayer. It is to pray, and my concentration on what I am doing is not a distraction from prayer but part of what makes what I am doing prayer. The Eucharistic prayer feels to me a love song addressed to God which, on behalf of us all, I am privileged to read and sing. I am also aware that, although women have been ordained priests in the Episcopal Church for more than thirty years, to see a woman at the altar still, for many women, mediates acceptance.

The Christmas that followed my ordination, to my regret I had no part as a priest in the liturgy because Jim and I were once more in New York. But during Lent and Holy Week, one of St. Paul's priests was recovering from surgery, and so I was needed. The day before Palm Sunday, Lowell called to ask me to chant the Blessing of the Palms, which is not easy to sing; he had a cold. On Tuesday of Holy Week, I presided at the Eucharist as Lowell was still coughing. Wednesday there were services at St. Martin's, and then Lowell taught me how to cense the altar in preparation for Easter. I preached on Maundy Thursday, and that night, for the first time, Lowell and I washed each other's feet.

At the end of the service, Lowell and I removed the reserved sacrament from the aumbry and extinguished the aumbry candle. We had stripped the altar of its hangings and washed the altar, slowly and reverently, in symbolic anticipation of the death of Christ. The ritual washing of the altar continues to be for me one of the most moving events of the church year. To minister to the dying Christ is for me, I know, to minister also to my mother. It is to do the sort of thing which many years ago I was considered too young to do. It is to do what my aunt did at the mortuary when she combed out my mother's hair.

Then on Good Friday, I led the prayers at the foot of the cross. At the long Easter vigil on Saturday night, I read St. John Chrysostom's sermon, the traditional sermon for that service, which welcomes all to the feast. I returned to St. Paul's on Easter morning to preside at 8:45, having slept at most three hours. Afterward, I expected to go home, but Lowell asked me to stay. He knew that the crowd at 11 o'clock would be just as large.

Holy Week does not appear on the university's calendar. On Maundy Thursday, besides teaching my classes, I was on the committee for a thesis defense. I would not want Holy Week and Easter to be always so intense, not while I am still at the university, and they have not been so, but I was grateful to be so immersed in the liturgy that first spring. Just before my ordination, my friend Sr. Carolyn of St. Margaret's had said, "Lynne, in order to celebrate the Eucharist, you must make your life more contemplative, more spacious." I have not yet accomplished that. But when I mentioned it to Lowell, his reply went to the heart of priesthood: "If you can do it, do it for us all."

Chapter 18

When I was young, I was embarrassed that Ed was my brother. I feared my friends would think badly of me because of him. His body would go rigid, and he would vocalize hooting sounds. His temper tantrums were terrible and his behavior outside social norms. My brother had frequent episodes of grand mal epilepsy, and I found the convulsions frightening. He took a lot of our mother's attention, which made me jealous and angry, but my lack of compassion for him left her upset with me. Mother never acknowledged that Ed would not be normal. To her death, she maintained he would "catch up." But when Ed could not be enrolled in kindergarten, he began to seem irredeemably different to me.

The psychiatric evaluation reads "moderate mental retardation and obsessive-compulsive disorder." Ed was three when he learned to walk and six before he started to speak. When our mother died, Ed was living at the School for the Blind. His eyesight is very poor. At the end of that academic year, the staff told Dad that Ed could not continue there. They declared that his behavior had become unmanageable.

The tensions in the household were almost unbearable even with Ed away, and they got worse when he moved home. At Amy's insistence that he had to be made to mind, once Dad beat him. Amy, in order to control him, used to herd him around by poking with a yardstick at his feet. As my memories of these things surfaced in therapy, the mental images came up like vomit. Sabra hypothesized that Ed was being so stubborn because he was grieving Mother's death. That Ed might have been grieving had never crossed my mind, and I was astounded. I am sure that neither Dad nor Amy ever thought of that.

Chapter 18

Two years later Ed was admitted to the state institution for the mentally retarded, a decision Dad and Amy took reluctantly. Beatrice is a hundred miles from Omaha, but they continued to bring him home for every holiday. Until almost the end of their lives, they visited him every three or four weeks. At the time Ed was admitted, the facility for the mentally retarded was a terrifying place. The upper story porch of the M building was surrounded by chicken wire. Its purpose was to keep the residents from falling, but to me it looked like a prison fence. I used to watch the men leaning against the wire in the summer's heat, vocalizing and moaning. There was nothing for them to do.

Ed was placed on the men's ward, an open room lined with beds, even though he was a puny thirteen year old. The institution was overcrowded, underfunded, understaffed, and unregulated. One holiday Ed came home with two black eyes from "falling." On another occasion, after piecing together what Ed was saying, my parents concluded that he was being sexually abused by an attendant. At the end of each visit, whenever it was time for our family to return to Omaha, Ed would crawl into the footwell of the car and refuse to get out. Once my parents discovered that a resident had taken a cigarette and burned it into every vertebra in Ed's back.

As an adolescent, I took these things in with a feeling of dull helplessness. For many years I had nightmares of running through the corridors of those buildings. In my dreams they loomed many times their actual size. I dreamed that I was unable to find Ed, and I dreamed that I was imprisoned and trying to escape. Sometime around 1970 (it was after I had moved away from Nebraska and so I do not know the details) a class action lawsuit and federal regulation brought change. Fearing that the alternatives might be even worse, Dad, as Ed's guardian, made an agonized, and in retrospect probably wise, decision to opt out of the class action lawsuit. The lawsuit brought community placement for many of the residents, and the renamed "Beatrice State Developmental Center" became a significantly different place. Ed now lives in a house-like "living unit" with fifteen other men, where he and a roommate share a room. The long-abandoned M building was demolished for a parking lot.

Ed empties the trash from wastebaskets all over the campus. He likes his work, and he is paid. There is an indoor swimming pool which he enjoys, and a van takes residents on frequent outings for shopping and recreation. The staff members I have met are caring people. Pat, who for a long time was his teacher, had a genuine rapport with him. Ed thought of her as a friend, and she seemed to think of him in that way too. For a while one of the nurses at BSDC happened to be a member of Christ Church Episcopal in Beatrice. After she heard how much he liked going there to church with me, she began taking Ed to church with her.

Christ Church Episcopal is small enough that any visitor is conspicuous. When the rector asked how I happened to be there, I explained that my brother was a resident of BSDC, and he proposed that I bring Ed along. I thought about the length of the service and the daunting complexity of Episcopal liturgy. I worried that Ed might not be quiet enough or need too many trips to the restroom. I knew Ed liked the Protestant services at BSDC, yet I had doubts, and so in Fayetteville I discussed the idea with Lowell, who had worked at a camp for the mentally handicapped. "Ed will love the liturgy. It works on so many levels below consciousness," Lowell said.

My brother was fascinated by the procession and the vestments, just as Lowell thought. Ed went with me to the altar rail where we received communion. Throughout the entire service, he remained still. Being greeted by parishioners did make him ill at ease, even more than I expected. Yet as we walked down the sidewalk, he said, "Thank you, Lynne," and the pleasure in his voice took me by surprise. When I returned from seminary, Ed wanted the prayer book open to the right page even though he cannot read. He mumbled along whenever the congregation would pray or sing. Since his hands shake, he received the bread on his tongue as he knelt at the communion rail. I guess Ed became, in spirit, an Episcopalian.

Doug and I considered whether we should try to bring Ed to Fayetteville for my ordination. To make two round trips to Nebraska seemed logistically impossible, and the social demands of the weekend would have been too great for him. Wanting Ed to be present was more than anything else our fantasy of completeness. Then a friend who was a pilot offered to fly Ed to Fayetteville for a weekend later on when I could have time with him. In the plane he squeezed my arm tightly all the way, yet he seemed more excited than scared. That Saturday I showed him where I work, and we rode the steam train in Eureka Springs, an Ozark tourist town. On Sunday morning I took Ed with me into the sacristy, and my friend sat with him while I presided at St. Paul's. The weekend seemed to me the completion of my ordination.

Ed said he'd had a "huge big time," and he still remembers going up in the plane. A year later I was invited to preach and preside at Christ Church in Beatrice, which I gladly did. One of Ed's and my favorite things to do was to drive around the Nebraska countryside in our Miata, top down (until we needed to trade it for a small pick-up truck). Another is to go to church together.

Being with Ed and attending his annual evaluations have been illuminative for me. When I asked his teacher if she could help him practice social skills for church, she described him as "shy," and I thought, "Of course!" Whenever we are out driving, he is relaxed until we turn back toward Beatrice, and then he talks incessantly. "That is separation anxiety," Sabra said. I know that I would not be able to live with Ed, but I feel distraught and vulnerable every time I return home. Attachment increases anxiety about loss for us both.

Ed's evaluations state that he cannot stand being teased or criticized, and I muse about which of us is being described. They say that, when he is criticized, he becomes anxious and agitated and self-destructive; he pinches himself and pulls on his ears. As a baby, Ed would bang his head against the wall, and even though I know there are medical reasons for infant head-banging, it remains for me an image of psychological pain. Meanwhile, self-understanding has helped me to understand my brother. Once I became aware of how "fear of a breakdown that has already happened" disrupts my conscious thought, I began to notice it also in Ed.

Doug says he cannot remember our mother, and Ed appears not to do so either. Nevertheless, as I watch how anxiety interrupts Ed's functioning, I think about how our mother's death must have affected him. I wonder whether, if he were being evaluated now, to the diagnosis would be added "posttraumatic stress." When Ed gets anxious, his fear about his inadequacy causes him to talk obsessively about cleaning his room. Though usually they are voiced only if I am alone, when I get anxious, my anxiety too erupts in obsessive thoughts. And as I began to pay attention to the content of those thoughts, I found that I was saying to myself over and over, "Lynne can't talk."

That mantra signaled the breaking through of fear, fear that I even now cannot fully articulate in words. And since, even had I found words, in my adolescence there was no one with whom to talk, that mantra expressed my isolation. Ed lacks vocabulary and abstract concepts. The psychiatric report says he has no capacity for insight, and he cannot put what he feels into words. Yet the brother that I in childhood saw as utterly different has become uncannily familiar. In Ed I encounter my unconscious self.

Dad and Amy used to worry that after their deaths Doug and I would not care what happened to Ed. They worried that we would be too far away and too busy with our own careers and families. Yet despite having two sons and living far away, Doug, Ed's legal guardian, visits him twice a year, as do I. In college I once said to a priest that my mother was dead and my brother in an institution—how could I believe in God? In the presence of suffering, theological answers have always seemed to me inadequate, even fatuous. Whenever I am pressed by another philosopher about how there could be an all-powerful and loving God in a world where there is suffering, I say I am not sure God is omnipotent. But within my own mind, as I grow older, it is the question that somehow recedes.

Chapter 19

At night the sound of breaking glass awakened me. I told Sabra I felt like a pot, its shards hurtling farther and farther apart. I was like a planet shattered by a comet in outer space. I began therapy looking forward to ordination. My intention was to have some conversations about CPE. But there was something I needed to know, something I was at last so close to knowing that I could not let it go. Eighteen months later, I understood my experience of my mother's death.

I explained to Sabra that a workman was crushed at the bottom of the hospital's elevator shaft while my mother was hospitalized. The hospital, black and airless and inescapable, was a place where life was crushed out. I remembered the title of a book my mother was reading, *Too Much, Too Soon*. My aunts took turns living in our household during Mother's illness. Their sister's breast cancer was a repetition of their own mother's illness and death during their adolescence, and it must have stirred their fears for their children and themselves. However, at the time I did not understand any of this. It seemed to me that my aunts were always in the kitchen, and yet the food did not taste good.

One of my aunts told me that my mother was very ill, and I must not make demands on her attention. I was insulted that she thought it necessary to tell me that. In therapy I finally began to understand the violent and self-punishing dreams and fantasies that had never ceased to haunt me. "When our needs cannot be met," Sabra said, "we blame ourselves for having the need." I had always thought of my mother's death as the beginning of my distress. Now I saw that in my mother's illness, I too was becoming ill.

For many years at night I have suffered from leg pains whose cause my doctor cannot find. In therapy I imagined myself, legs braced against the door resisting death. One night, half-asleep, I had a terrifying image of God as a thin edge, like the top of a cloud, and another time I thought of Bambi, standing over her dead mother after the forest fire. Sabra told me that these images are memories of how I conceptualized my mother's death.

Alone at night sometimes I would hear myself scream. The scream would arrive before awareness of the thought that triggered it. My blood pressure still spikes in the morning as I awaken every day to the unconscious shock of mother loss. When I saw my mother's body at the mortuary, I had no words, but in the midst of therapy, one night in an empty house I shouted: "Do you know what a dead body is like? I have seen dead birds, a dead cat, but never a dead body!" Sabra told me, "Sometimes first year medical students find the cadavers of persons they did not even know so distressing that they vomit."

Nearly a year and a half after therapy started, one night I dreamed I was standing over a teddy bear that lay next to a youngster in a bed. The bear was small and homemade, like one that, as an infant, I had been given. In my dream, the bear was so sad that his sadness filled my whole being. Surrounding his upper body was a beautiful silver hoop which, he said, was too much for him. "Ah, Bear, you are a beautiful Bear," I replied, and gently I showed him how the pajamas he was wearing covered his feet. Then I took my forefinger and ran it slowly and tenderly downward, starting at his nose. His belly was softer than velvet, so soft that, startled by the sensation, I awoke, the softness lingering on my fingertip. "Bearable, unbearable sadness," said Sabra, playing with words. Within days of that dream, I knew, in a way that left no doubt, what I believed about my mother's death.

It was late July, 2001, and Sabra and I were meeting almost every day. Jim was about to move back from New York, having settled his mother's estate. The inward focus I had maintained that summer clearly could not last, and it was as if a sense of urgency permeated even my unconscious. We were talking about the anger and shame and anxiety I to this day feel that, when I was a small child, my mother spanked me. I also happened to be reading a book on Melanie Klein, some of whose writings I knew from Ann's course. Klein had a visceral sense of the violence of childhood's feelings, and at night strange archaic images filled my dreams. One night I had a dream so chaotic and bizarre that it defied coherent narration. Neither Sabra nor I could make any sense of it, but walking home from her office, all at once I knew. It seems that anything, *anything*, was less fearful than the absolute powerlessness which had been my true condition. All at once I knew that I blamed myself for my mother's death.

I believed that my mother had died because I was not good enough. I believed that if I could be good enough, even now, she would not die. That this is what I believed is not surprising. It is precisely what Freud would have assumed. Moreover, the idea had years before been presented to me, casually, by a retreat leader who hardly knew me. It had been asserted, as a kind of given, by a substitute therapist I met only once. Yet theirs had been proposals I could not recognize as applying to me. They seemed remote possibilities. How can we be so opaque to ourselves? And what is it that lets what has been hidden be so clearly seen? What had until then been a mere hypothesis became that day a truth I cannot deny. I continued to see Sabra for several more months, but that July was the real terminus of therapy. I had found what I needed to know.

Years ago someone told me that I should "get on antidepressants and never get off." I do not presume to know what anyone else should do. I would not even want to say what I would do in other circumstances. But I am very glad that I did not take even the first part of that advice. I had learned in Ann's classes that dreams and obsessive thoughts are not nonsense but communication; they are "primary speech." I was fortunate in my choice of therapist and in having the means to persevere. I wanted relief from symptoms, but even more, I wanted psychological continuity with my past. What I wanted more than anything else was self-knowledge.

Looking back a number of years later, what I learned about myself has blessed my life immensely, letting me experience the joy of ordinary time. The thoughts and images that so troubled me come much less often and less intensely. The interruptions of consciousness which Winnicott's "Fear of Breakdown" made conscious enough that I was able to count their occurrence (one day I found they were happening many times a minute) now most days hardly happen at all.

Nevertheless, my mother's death is still inextricably in me. It is in my brain cells and my muscles and my bones. The panic that breaks through my conscious thought can be triggered by the season or by funerals and in less foreseeable ways. One summer morning I watched as Casey, then a puppy, lost his favorite water toy off the side of our dock in twenty feet of water. He had chewed his ball so much that its buoyancy was gone. Casey ran up and down the dock in agitation, unable to understand what was happening. Then he jumped into the water and swam round and round where his ball had last been seen until, fearing for his safety, I called him back to the shore. Although he soon got interested in other things, the agitated feeling of loss lingered for me the rest of the day. Michael Eigen, another psychoanalyst whose work I read in Ann's courses, wrote that from therapy one learns to abandon the search for perfection. Part of what therapy accomplishes is tolerance for oneself.

Chapter 19

As soon as I returned to Fayetteville after seminary, Jim moved into his mother's house in Brooklyn for what would turn out to be two and a half years. For eighteen months he took care of his mother. Then after her death, he repaired and sold her house and settled her estate. I went back to New York for every vacation during the time that he was there. I felt a lot of anxiety for Jim while he was living in Brooklyn; he was depressed. And the hardest part for us both was not knowing how long caring for his mother might go on.

As the months went by, some of our friends in Fayetteville thought that Jim was saintly, and others thought he was crazy. His mother refused even to consider a nursing home, and Jim's decision to take care of her expressed his concern for her. It also reflected her manipulative disregard for his life. Of course, had Jim cared less about what she thought of him, he would have found confronting her easier. As with us all, his strength and his vulnerability are intertwined. Years before when we were in marriage counseling, Jim said he could see that I still carried within me my mother's death and my troubled relationship with my father and stepmother. When he added that his relationship with his parents was fine, what seemed to me his obtuseness made me furious. During his mother's illness, Jim came to see himself and his mother more realistically. Then late in the summer of 2001, finally, he moved home.

I do not think we ever wondered whether, after eleven years apart, we might find living together difficult. We were happy to be together, and because I was beginning a sabbatical, we were together a lot. Twenty-some years ago, as we trailered our small Laser sailboat to Beaver Lake, about an hour away, we used to dream of having a weekend house. Land is relatively affordable in Arkansas, and even before Jim moved back to Fayetteville, we used my inheritance to buy property on Beaver Lake.

Spring brings rain, a carpet of tiny wildflowers on the rocky ledges, and migrating songbirds. In summer I swim off our dock and am glad for the cool breeze that most evenings rises from the lake. In the fall the woods turn yellow, brown, and red, and then the leaves tumble, opening vistas of the hills. In winter the cold on the north side of the hill, our side of the hill, penetrates our boots and woolen socks. Here the restlessness that at midlife took me to Cambridge and then Grandchamp and New York City has entirely vanished. This is where I want to be. And this is where we have built a house.

Like nearly everyone who has ever built a house, Jim and I did not know quite what we were getting into. When he first saw the property, Jim worried, with good reason, whether the site was too steep for a road. Building took longer and cost more than we ever imagined it could, and by choice, but also necessity, we did what we could do ourselves. While Jim was still in New York, we began sketching a not so big post and beam house with an open floor plan. We wanted a lot of glass on the lake-facing side beneath a shed roof that would rise toward the lake. A knowledgeable and sympathetic dealer for Lindal Cedar Homes drew up the plans, and Lindal did the engineering and supplied the materials. Even so, we did not know enough to understand that the direction of the roof beams we insisted on would greatly complicate installation of the ductwork for heating and cooling. We did not know that aesthetic simplicity and what is economical to build are not the same.

Except for the window arrangement and a stairway, we did not consult an architect. We made a full-size cardboard mock-up of the freestanding soapstone fireplace that divides the living and dining room spaces, and in fact we modeled everything we could. As the house emerged, we were amazed at how well we did. I admired the skill of our builder and the subcontractors who worked on the project. Whenever I became irritable that construction was so slow (even now there are still things to be done), Jim would remind me that the present is to be treasured and that our problems are small. Those years brought the death of our next door neighbor in Fayetteville, one of my colleagues in the philosophy department, poet Jim Whitehead who encouraged me to write this book, and John Harrison, the retired head of the university's library, who audited my Merton class. All of them were more or less our age. One of the last things John did in his life was to urge us to get a dog.

"When you smell like the dog and you are as dirty as the dog and the dog is in your lap, that kind of openness to another species is what Merton means by openness to God," John said in class one day. Jim and I remembered Mopsy and Goliath and all they had meant in our lives. We had forgotten the difference between a puppy and a dog. Casey is beautiful and bright and affectionate and good-natured and fun. He is perfectly matched to the lake and the woods. He loves to swim. But over the phone my friend Renee in Michigan laughed, "I cannot believe you would take on a puppy when your house is still in construction!" By the calendar Casey is now years past puppyhood, but sometimes it seems to me I still spend half my day trying to wear out the dog.

House building, a Golden Retriever puppy, the long-ago death of my mother, the renewal of a marriage, the recent death of friends—"Alice," Jim said when years ago he read a chapter of this manuscript, "you think you are writing about religion, but it is really about life." But this is what I think incarnation means: that God is in ordinary life.

Chapter 20

Jim had noticed the sailplane at an air show that summer (this was the year before seminary). The Illini Gliding Club offered rides on Saturdays for a modest fee. To persuade me, he said, "It is like sailing but in three dimensions." The next morning I was sitting in front of a pilot high over central Illinois in formation with the tow plane. Then at 2300 feet just beneath a bank of clouds, the tow cord was released. It is eerie to drift silently through the sky, without an engine. Gliders are kept aloft by their long and slender wings.

Our shadow passed over the high school, and the baseball diamond, then across fields of corn and the factory yard where rolls of wire lay strewn like bales of hay. When the pilot told me how to use the stick and rudder, my palms were sweaty, and my stomach was queasy as he let me fly.

Later that morning I would stand on the runway as Jim was aloft. There I thought of the birds' way of being. Memories and daydreams, times past and times possible, alongside the present, seemed to float. "I pray that you may have the power to comprehend, with all the saints, what is the breadth and length and height and depth," wrote Paul (or whoever was the author of Ephesians). Do we live, so routinely that we scarcely notice, like submarines beneath the sky?

Sometimes while I was living in New York, I would walk to the Lower East Side for the Saturday night vigil at the Russian Orthodox cathedral. There the altar was hidden behind the iconostasis, a screen of icons. If art stands between us and what is represented and calls attention to itself, icons are not art. They are intended to be transparent, once their symbolism is grasped. Icons are meant not to be seen but to be seen through to eternity. The iconostasis is a meeting place between heaven and earth.

For Plato what is visible and changing is an image of the eternal and unchanging. It is the Forms which are most real, and they are not the world we see. Plato insisted that those who would study philosophy first master mathematics. Mathematics could be called a meeting place between the visible and the invisible, between earth and heaven. "Be present, O merciful God, and protect us through the hours of this night, so that we who are wearied by the changes and chances of this life may rest in your eternal changelessness." In this ancient collect for compline in the Book of Common Prayer, the place where earth and heaven meet is sleep.

When Jim and I were living apart, he used to tell me to call him in the middle of the night if I was having trouble sleeping. One night I called him in central Illinois at 3 a.m. "Alice, just think of the distance from the house to here as a very large room, 535 miles long. What separates us is only space, and if that is all that separates us, that is not so bad." To stand before the iconostasis, to reverence the icons and pray, was to see myself, here and now, living in the presence of God and the saints. Whether the temporal is embedded in the eternal is a different question from whether, for us individually, there is anything after death. But it is natural enough to suppose that if God's life is eternal, there might be eternal life for us also, and many religious traditions have held that it is so. In Christianity, that hope is grounded in the Resurrection.

I have a hypothesis about the resurrection appearances. It is that the narratives stand to the experiences which underlie them as dream narratives stand to dreams. I do not mean that I think the disciples' experiences were visions. I do not know what their experiences were. My hypothesis is only about the relationship between the narratives and the experiences they describe. Anyone who has ever tried to tell someone else about a dream must know what I mean when I say that dreams are one thing and dream narratives another. The narrative has structure and greater conceptual clarity. Even if the sense of the uncanny that often characterizes the sorts of dreams we long remember is still evident in the narrative, some of the elusiveness, the "feel" of the dream, has been lost.

For the experiences I have had that I think of as experiences of God, words often seem to give them too much precision. As I try to write or talk about my experiences of God, the content becomes more definite. When I try to put words to it, the experience takes on a form, and sometimes I resort to phrases like "it was as if . . ." In the Gospel accounts of the resurrection appearances, what I see is an attempt to put something elusive, too strange to be described, into words. Yet whatever those narratives have been unable to explain, they nonetheless capture the disciples' sense of being in the presence of the holy.

But then the Resurrection, whatever it was, was not just something that happened to Jesus—some odd, even miraculous event; something happened to the disciples too. Their experience, whatever it was, must have been frightening and disorienting, but it was also empowering and it was healing. Jesus was dead, and yet he was in some way there with them. "When it was evening on that day, the first day of the week, and the doors of the house where the disciples had met were locked…, Jesus came and stood among them and said, 'Peace be with you.'" The resurrection stories are full of appearances and disappearances, and they are in their effect like the reappearance of a mother to her infant. The resurrection appearances let the disciples learn that there was stability beneath their loss.

In the Resurrection, the disciples discovered God's love to have consequences greater than anything they could imagine. The Resurrection taught the disciples that the conflicted and imperfect choices of human history could be redeemed. They learned that there could be redeeming of things they had done. They found that things that had been done to them could be healed. God gives life to the dead, to what was dead in each of them. God was calling into existence things that were not. Having met Jesus on the road, they recognized him when at supper he took bread, blessed and broke it, and gave it to them. In the Eucharist we say that the body and blood of our Lord Jesus Christ will keep us all in everlasting life. The bread and wine are visible means for learning to know and trust that what is invisible—the spiritual body and blood of Christ—is real.

To see experience in this way is to trust that in life and in death, we live in relationship to God and to one another. It is to see ourselves as living in relationship not just to our thoughts of one another. Memory, after all, was the cause of the disciples' grief and loneliness and despair. It is to see ourselves as living not just in relationship to the effects of others' lives on ours, but really living in relationship to one another, both in their presence and in their absence. In the burial office, when prayer is offered for those we love and see no longer, it is offered for those we *love*, present tense, and as a priest I sometimes remind myself that every Eucharist is celebrated in the presence of all the angelic hierarchies of heaven. Yet I do often have to make an effort to remember. I suspect that how we feel about death depends a lot on when in our lives, and how, we have experienced loss.

Although I am a priest, my experience of loss makes the idea of a wholeness that encompasses life and death seem like fantasy. I do not know how I would feel about my own death if I knew it were imminent, but I know how I feel about the death of those I care about, especially when death comes too soon. I still want to be able to talk with my mother, if only by phone. Everything in me objects, deeply, to absence where there was once a particular, irreplaceable, presence. Everything in me rebels against irreversible loss.

That is a truth that comes from my own experience. Yet what is less clear is what I should conclude from my experience. What is its relationship to the truth? It could be that the extremity of my need for things to be other than they are keeps me from accepting that death is the end. Or it could be, could it not, that my experience of devastating loss just makes it extraordinarily difficult for me to believe that there really is resurrection?

In our empirically minded age, perhaps most of us sometimes suspect that death is the end, but in *Foundations of Christian Faith*, Karl Rahner, a 20th century Catholic theologian, protested: "But a few other things also existed previously [besides the biological system]: a person with love, fidelity, pain, responsibility, freedom. By what right really does one maintain that everything is over? Why should it really be 'over.' Because we do not notice anything any more? This argument seems a little weak! All that really follows from it is that the deceased no longer exists for me, the survivor."

To argue that a lack of evidence for something does not disprove it is a method of arguing that is sure to lead to a lot of false conclusions. But Rahner's point is a different one: whether not seeing should lead to the conclusion that something is not the case depends on what it is we do not see. "Becoming ceases when being begins, and we do not notice anything of it because we ourselves are still in the process of becoming," Rahner wrote. Just because we do not notice anything anymore, should we expect to?

I want truth about whether there is a God and about the meaning of life and what happens at death. I do not want to be deceived. But our longings for God, and for those we love and have lost, could they be, as Rahner thought, rumors of resurrection? Plato's third century C.E. pagan follower Plotinus thought that our very capacity for longing tells us something about Reality and not just about ourselves. Plotinus took our longing to mean that the true home of our souls, the home of our true selves, is There. However much of beauty and goodness Plotinus saw in the world (and he did see its goodness and beauty), he thought it was not the ultimate Beauty, the ultimate Good. And even when Plotinus did undervalue the world we see, which he sometimes did, the value of his question remains: do our longings tell us something about what is Real?

When I am asked what my faith in God is about, I reply that it is trust, or at least a desire to trust, that our longings are not tragic but purposeful. My hope is that they are present in order to lead us into love and into truth. Although we, like the disciples, are not able to see in an unambiguous way the larger life for which we long, perhaps we do sometimes see intimations of a creation grounded in eternity. For me some of those intimations come in the liturgy. To celebrate the Eucharist tugs at the curtain of my experience of loss.

Chapter 21

I ache when I encounter students who suffer because of what they have been taught about God. What they say often reminds me of the parable in Matthew in which the king burned the city because his intended guests disdained his invitation to a wedding banquet. The king next invited street people, but when one of those who came was not wearing a wedding robe, he ordered the man bound hand and foot and thrown into the outer darkness. Scholars say that, when the angry king burns the city, the parable is referring to the destruction of Jerusalem in 70 C.E., in which case, presumably, the parable did not come from Jesus. They believe that the king's anger at those for whom the feast had been prepared, but who ask to be excused and then dare to kill his messengers, refers to the Jews. That a guest invited in from the street is thrown out because of his attire is, they say, meant for the church as an apocalyptic warning.

Of course, the king's monstrous behavior is intended to be caricature. But whatever the writer of Matthew thought, how can we think that God burned Jerusalem, or let the Romans do it, as a judgment against the Jews for rejecting Christ? As for the casting out of the man not wearing wedding garb (any clean robe, scholars say), I think of how, at General Seminary in New York, I would frequently walk past Holy Apostles Episcopal Church. Eight blocks from the seminary, the parish staff of Holy Apostles included a chef and his assistant, the sous-chef. At 11 a.m. each weekday morning, the line for the soup kitchen went all the way around the block. Many of the folks who came to the church-run soup kitchens struggled with substance abuse and untreated mental illness. They were people, many of whom had been abused and some of whom had prison records, who were living on the streets. It was unimaginable that anyone in that line of guests outside Holy Apostles would be refused because he or she was not wearing clean clothes.

In the seventeenth century, Anglican philosopher and theologian Benjamin Whichcote, one of the Cambridge Platonists, argued, "... if the creature [God] hath made be finite and fallible, He must give him allowance..." For Whichcote, "There is that in God that is more beautiful than power...," namely, God's goodness. Whichcote was arguing that views of God which do not even conform to the reasonableness and moral reliability expected of human beings have to be wrong.

Whichcote's words were written in the context of disputes about predestination, but they apply equally well to interpretations of the atonement. There is no doctrine of the atonement in Christianity, only many metaphors, including ransom and victory in a cosmic battle. In the Book of Common Prayer, the contemporary Eucharistic prayer describes Christ's death as "a perfect sacrifice for the whole world." The more Elizabethan version of the prayer begins: "All glory be to thee, Almighty God...for that thou, of thy tender mercy, didst give thine only Son Jesus Christ to suffer death upon the cross for our redemption; who made there, by his one oblation of himself once offered, a full, perfect, and sufficient sacrifice, oblation, and satisfaction for the sins of the whole world."

Sometimes the atonement has been taken to mean the propitiation of a wrathful deity and sometimes the expiation of our sins through a vicarious restitution, a kind of reparation or making amends. But no one can make restitution to himself, not even God, and so the idea seems incoherent. To be sure, God the Son is thought to be distinct in some way from God the Father, and so perhaps Christ could accomplish restitution if the Father accepted his torture and death to be such. But what kind of God would do this? Even if, as is commonly said, it is not a matter of reconciling God to us, but us to God, how could crucifixion be the means? Who would worship a God who thinks in such terms? Who would desire that Christ, an innocent victim, suffer on their behalf?

One day in seminary as my theology professor and I were talking on the way to lunch, she asked me what I would say was the reason for the crucifixion. Intentionally, I took "the reason" to mean "the cause" and I replied, "Christ was crucified because people got mad at him." In Jesus' particular circumstances, crucifixion may have been the inevitable consequence of a faithful life, and the faithfulness of his life, even in extreme suffering, matters to us. But I do not think the crucifixion accomplished our salvation in the sense that it was some sort of transaction. I do not think the crucifixion had a purpose in that sense.

The stark reality of crucifixion used to leave me with such a sense of futility that the jubilant mood of Easter year after year seemed unreal. The all too graphic Good Friday services stir up my own deadening trauma, and I have stopped going to church on Good Friday. On the other hand, in the Maundy Thursday service, I find layer upon layer of meaning. In the Gospel for Maundy Thursday, when Jesus had finished washing the disciples' feet, he asked them, "Do you know what I have done to you?" When Jesus washed their feet, his action was expressive, and what it expresses is how God feels about us.

When we see God exemplified in Christ, what we come to know is God's compassion. When we see humanity exemplified in Christ, what we see in Christ is how, with unobstructed awareness of God's love, humanity would be. On the cross Jesus said, "Father, forgive them for they know not what they are doing." Told that unless Jesus washed his feet, he would not share in what Jesus is revealing, at the last supper Peter exclaimed, "Lord, not my feet only but also my hands and head!" Yet the Peter who proclaimed his devotion to Christ but hours later betrayed him, and the crowds that days before welcomed Jesus with palm branches shouted "Crucify him!" Often we do not know what we are doing.

In *Showings*, the fourteenth century mystic St. Julian of Norwich described a series of visions on which she had meditated for twenty years. The central vision is the allegory of a Lord and a Servant. It is a vision that reveals to Julian why there is no anger in God. The servant runs off eagerly to do his Lord's will, and because of his inexperience, in his very eagerness he stumbles and falls. Lying injured on the ground, the servant is in too much pain to be able to look up and see his Lord's concern for him. Believing he has let his Lord down, the servant is worried that his Lord might be angry. The servant fears that his Lord has abandoned him.

The servant's condition is Peter's and Judas' and Pilate's and the crowd's condition. It is our human condition. In the substance of our souls, Julian said, we *are* united to God. Christ's Passion cannot reestablish that union because it is a bond that has never been lost. Yet while God knows the faithfulness of love for God that is in us, we do not know ourselves, and so we do not always see our desire for what it really is.

What we really want is to love God and to be loved by God, but we do not always recognize that. And we do not always know that the love of God is something we already have. Instead, in our anxiety and confusion we try to find other ways to satisfy the longing whose nature we do not understand. We attempt to accumulate for ourselves power that is not rightfully ours or success or status or possessions or pleasurable experiences, whatever we think it will take to make us invulnerable, important, lovable, and happy. We desire whatever we think it will take to make gods of ourselves. It seems to me that sin is the effect of despair, a despair that is caused by misdiagnosed longing. And our longing causes despair because of our profound misreading of God and of ourselves.

So when Jesus washed his disciples' feet, he was showing them that they did not have to make themselves into something they could not be in order to love God and be loved by God. He was teaching them that God loves what is less than God, and so we need not be afraid. That is why Jesus is the Christ, the source of our salvation. The "atonement" is to be found in his manner of life. I believe that Christ is our pattern and our teacher.

To let someone wash our feet is to let someone be as Christ to us. To let our feet be washed is to acknowledge that the meaning of our lives is not to be found in the sum total of our accomplishments or failures. To let our feet be washed is to be awakened to the knowledge that we are lovable and we are loved. It is to be awakened to the awareness that our deepest desire is for God and that what we most desire is not something we lack but something we have. To let our feet be washed is to see ourselves as God sees us, but to see ourselves as God sees us is to see one another as God does. It is to know the beauty of our neighbor's soul, beautiful in its longing for God, even if that longing goes unacknowledged. And the recognition of the beauty that is hidden in one another is the ground of compassion.

Several years before 9/11 in a church basement in New York, the children had expressed their fears about the world around them. They were afraid of being alone. They worried about the violence of war and the violence in their schools and neighborhoods. Some of them thought about pollution, and the climate, and endangered species. Those children were not so sure they would like growing up. And one of them was afraid—I do not know what movies were playing at the time, but one youngster was afraid—of being eaten.

The children in that classroom knew a lot, much more than kids should have to know. They knew the vulnerability of the young and the defenseless. They knew our society's ills and also the dangers, some of which we have created, in the natural world. And that child was right to be worried about monsters. We have learned over and over that we can become monsters in our behavior toward one another and the world's other creatures. We are now beginning to recognize that we must no longer allow ourselves to be monsters who scorch and devour the earth itself.

I have seen in medieval cathedrals carvings of a mother pelican hammering her beak into her breast. Christ is being depicted as a Mother Pelican because, in times of drought, the female pelican was thought to feed her brood with her blood. In the Eucharist, the bread and wine become spiritually the body and blood of Christ, and what is spiritual is real. Our fears are turned upside down and inside out in Holy Week. We fear being eaten, and Christ says, "Feed on me."

Chapter 22

In the *Theaetetus* Plato wrote, "That is why a man should make all haste to escape from earth to heaven; and escape means becoming as like God as possible." Human beings become like God when they become just and pure, with understanding, Plato explained. In the ancient world, these lines, whose connection with the rest of the *Theaetetus* is not obvious, were the most quoted lines in Plato. They met with the approval of pagan and Christian writers alike. In the Christian tradition "becoming like God" means becoming like Christ. But what does it mean to be like Christ?

The church fathers believed that, in Jesus, creation is seen in its glorified state, and that is why Jesus could walk on water. In Corinthians Paul calls Jesus the "first fruits" of creation; as Jesus is, so all creation will be. That Christ became like us that we might be like him is explicit in 2 Peter, where it is said that we may become participants of the divine nature. It is implicit in Paul's view about human incorporation into Christ through the work of the Holy Spirit and in John's Letters and in much of the Gospel of John. "Beloved, we are God's children now; what we will be has not yet been revealed. What we do know is this: when he is revealed, we will be like him." That is from the First Letter of John.

In a bookshop in Cambridge, I came across a short scholarly book, now out of print, whose title was *Participation in God: A Forgotten Strand in Anglican Tradition*. The author discussed Anglicanism's greatest theologian Richard Hooker, the sermons of Lancelot Andrewes, Charles Wesley's hymns, and the Oxford Movement of liturgical retrieval. Two years later when I happened to meet Canon Allchin at Grandchamp, I told him how much I liked his book. He replied that he wished he had made it longer.

Participation in God is the most radically hopeful view of what human life is about that I can imagine. Yet neither classical philosophers nor post-Reformation theologians were naïve. When Plato urged us to become like God, just and pure and with understanding, he knew that the Athenians had massacred the male population of the island of Melos and taken the women and children as slaves, simply because the inhabitants of Melos refused to renounce their neutrality between Sparta and Athens. That had happened just a generation before during the Peloponnesian War.

Boethius' *The Consolation of Philosophy* is a sixth century Christian Platonist classic that sums up the wisdom of the ancient world. In it, Lady Philosophy argues that only the good are powerful. Because they do not achieve what they truly want, the wicked are always weak. What all human beings want, Lady Philosophy says, is happiness, by which she means not so much an emotion as human flourishing, and the weakness of the wicked is that they do not recognize where happiness can be found. What the wicked fail to see, she explains, is that our happiness is to become as God.

The claim that evildoers are powerless goes strongly against evidence that anyone, then or now, can see. In fact, Lady Philosophy's speech is addressed to Boethius (its author), who has been unjustly accused of treason. Boethius wrote his masterpiece while he was in prison waiting to be tortured to death. Lady Philosophy is not telling him that this will not happen. She is not saying that he should take comfort in a clean conscience or that pain does not matter or that after death all will be made well. She is talking about how without goodness we fail in our humanity. And if we fail in our humanity, she argues, we fail to be human beings.

For both Plato and Boethius, all of us long for the salvation that brings into being our true humanity. It is as we are drawn to the Good that salvation is found. In Book II of the *Confessions*, St. Augustine, another Christian Platonist, tried to analyze how other things could even seem more attractive: "Pride wears the mask of loftiness of spirit, although You alone, O God, are high over all." "Ignorance and sheer stupidity hide under the names of simplicity and innocence." "Sloth pretends that it wants quietude, but what sure rest is there save the Lord?" "Avarice wants to possess overmuch: but You possess all. Enviousness claims that it strives to excel: but what can excel before You?" Augustine's conclusion is this: "Even those who go from You and stand up against You are still perversely imitating You."

Plato thought it was because we fail in knowledge that we imitate the Good so badly. St. Augustine's ideas about free will and grace became so tangled that a wide variety of positions have been associated with his name, and scholars disagree about whether he changed his mind or ever had a coherent view. Two centuries before Augustine, St. Irenaeus proposed an idea I find attractive. Instead of reading the story of Adam and Eve as the story of a "Fall" from some earlier state in which they were as God intended human beings to be, he thought that Adam and Eve were inevitably childish because they were newly created. Irenaeus saw humanity as still lacking in experience.

In his essay "After ten years: a Reckoning made at New Year 1943," Dietrich Bonhoeffer reflected on the value of experience: "As time is the most valuable thing that we have, because it is the most irrevocable, the thought of any lost time troubles us whenever we look back. Time lost is time in which we have failed to live a full human life, gain experience, learn, create, enjoy, and suffer; it is time that has not been filled up, but left empty." He then added, "These last years have certainly not been like that. Our losses have been great and immeasurable, but time has not been lost." Somehow Bonhoeffer was able to write these lines from prison after ten futile years of opposition to Hitler.

I do believe that, just by being part of creation, we are invited to live and grow in love in the world that exists. For me, that world includes my mother's death. Yet if we do not make room for what is other than the way we would have things be, what we want is a world that is the fulfillment of our fantasies. If we do not will the otherness of others, what we really want is a world that is part of ourselves.

To want a world that is matched to our fantasies is not to love the world. Certainly to love a fantasy is not really to love oneself. Real love of ourselves requires the acceptance of ourselves as other, as other than our fantasized selves. It is to accept our particularity, our weakness, our vulnerability. And if love is the way in which we are to be like the God whose love is deeply God's own, then our love needs to be deeply our own. And perhaps our love is most deeply our own if it is, as Irenaeus thought, something that we come to from experience.

The twentieth century philosopher and mystic Simone Weil described creation as God's renunciation; whatever God creates is different from and less than God alone. The renunciation which comes from our love of God she called "decreation." For Weil the accent was on loss of self. For Boethius it was on the fulfillment of self. Both are expressions of the paradox familiar from the Gospels: "Those who lose their life for my sake . . . will save it." "Loss of self" and "fulfillment of self" reflect all the ambiguities which are part of our thinking about who we are.

Years ago I happened to see reproductions of some curious illuminated medieval manuscripts. In them, John, the beloved disciple, is shown as the creator holding the world. When on the cross Christ saw his mother standing with the disciple whom he loved, he said to Mary, "Here is your son," and to John, "Here is your mother." In giving them to one another, tradition held that Jesus made John the adopted Son of God, and what "St. John the Divine" was thought to have received by his adoption was Christ's divine nature. In ancient and medieval Christian theology, the role of creator was assigned to Christ the Logos rather than to God the Father. Putting these ideas together, John, as Christ's substitute, became the creator holding the world.

In depicting John as holding the world, time has been collapsed into eternity. John is portrayed as it was thought all of us will be. The definitive study of "theosis" or deification is Norman Russell's *The Doctrine of Deification in the Greek Patristic Tradition*, and Russell distinguishes several versions of theosis. In one of these, the change in us will be somehow ontological; without coming to share in God's essence, we will nevertheless take on certain divine properties, such as incorruptibility. But for Gregory of Nyssa, for example, the focus was on traits of character instead. What would creation be if humanity continued to grow in wisdom and courage and love, becoming increasingly like the Christ who was said to be more than can be humanly expressed? If we were able to believe that all of us will become as much like God in our capacity to love as the one who was to be called the Son of God, we would see ourselves and one another very differently. In the meantime, there is stability in hope.

Chapter 23

A lonely place where friends could not follow, an unsignposted country where childhood's maps matched no features of terrain, a land without protection from which I could not return, not as I had come, I encountered wilderness in my mother's death. And by teaching me to pray, it was into this much too familiar place that Bill was sending me. Yet in any landscape, it is barefoot we can better feel the truth in things, and in a different season, I found a measure of self-knowledge and of peace. Re-experiencing the wilderness also called into question much of my thinking about God and the nature of the self.

With therapy, I began to see in my feelings memories of earlier experiences. Whether modifiable or not, my emotions came to seem both more peculiarly mine and more explicable. I learned that their meaning was deeper than initially it had seemed. But if this life that wells up within me is part of me, then part of me had been, and doubtless still is, concealed. "Our movements, our stillness, the expressions on our faces, our tone of voice, our actions, what we dream and daydream, as well as what we actually put into words say who and what we are. To pray is to listen to and hear this self who is speaking," wrote Ann and Barry Ulanov in the opening paragraphs of *Primary Speech*, their book on prayer. Who is the self that is speaking, and why should one call listening to that self "prayer"? Here is one ancient proposal. In the fourth century, St. Gregory of Nyssa claimed that we are "mingled with God."

Gregory argued against Eunomius that words are signposts pointing us toward what is hidden. He thought that we cannot know the essence of anything in creation; we cannot fully know ourselves. If we cannot even know creation, how can we know God's essence? Gregory's answer was that we cannot. Of human thought, Gregory said that it is "neither keen-sighted enough to see clearly what is invisible, nor yet so far withheld from approach as to be unable to catch some faint glimpse of what it seeks to know." The properties we attribute to God, Gregory claimed, are a "conception."

Even if all we ever have is a conception of God, for Gregory this did not mean that we cannot increase our understanding of God. He held that as we come to know more of God, our conceptions improve. The way we come to know more of God is, for Gregory as for other Christian Platonists, by becoming more like God, and he thought we become more like God as we grow in goodness. Before Gregory, God had been supposed to be finite (in Greek philosophy, "infinite" meant what was indefinite or amorphous). But Gregory conceived of the infinite as inexhaustible, and he argued that God is infinite.

With the infinite, there is always an infinite yet to be traversed, Gregory argued. If God is infinite, our coming to know the divine is a process that will never, in all eternity, reach its end. In Philippians it is said that we need always to be "straining forward to what lies ahead," and Gregory took this to mean that whatever we know of God kindles our desire to know more. The process that Gregory described is something like striving to become a better and better athlete or musician. Progress brings real satisfaction and joy even as we know we will not reach, or even understand, perfection.

Gregory's belief that we can progress toward God without prior knowledge of the goal makes a lot of sense to me. It is what I experience in the act of writing. I do not begin with a clear idea of what I want to say and exactly how to say it. I write so that I have something to rewrite. And even when I do not have a sense of what it is that I am seeking, I can tell whether the revision is better. It is through rewriting that my knowledge of what I am trying to say starts to emerge.

In the beatitudes it is promised that the pure in heart will see God, and that seemed to promise the complete understanding Gregory believed we can never have. So this passage troubled Gregory, and his solution was to take the promise to mean that "the kingdom of God is within us." Gregory thought that, even after this life, we will not see God "face to face." Whoever has purified his heart, Gregory said, will perceive in his own inner beauty the image of the divine nature, and so the way we see God is by looking into ourselves.

"Those who contemplate the sun in a mirror, even though they do not look straight at the sun, see the sun no less in the ray in the mirror than do those who look directly at the circle of the sun," argued Gregory. When we see the sun in a mirror, for Gregory we do not see an image from which conclusions about the sun are drawn. What we see, however indirectly, is the sun. In other words, even though our seeing requires a medium, the mirror, it is not the image but what is imaged that we perceive.

So Gregory believed that, for each of us, insofar as we are purified, the self has a kind of transparency. What is seen is not the representation but that which it represents. In looking into ourselves to see God, we are seeing through ourselves, and that is why, changing his metaphor, Gregory could claim that we are "mingled with God." The beauty and goodness which we see are not only, or even primarily, our own.

For Plato, phenomena are images of the Forms, a metaphor that can suggest a separate realm for the eternal and unchanging, but Plato also described the relation of phenomena to Forms as their "participation" in the Forms. Similarly, Gregory wrote both of our being in the image of God and of our being mingled with God, where both are expressions of the same view. All our language for describing the relation of the world to God is metaphorical. And Gregory's belief that we cannot know God definitively seems to me to have much to commend it, as does his view that it is by becoming like God that we progress in knowing God. Yet the claim that we can recognize the better and are drawn to it presumes that there is a good to be recognized. For Gregory, just as for Plato, it is not our desire for something that makes that thing good.

The idea that there is good apart from our desires is often met with skepticism. To challenge particular teachings of their parents and clergy is for many students an ineluctable part of discovering themselves, as it should be. But having discovered how much variety there is among cultures, past and present, some of them tend to conclude, too hastily, I think, that there is only what they call good, or others call good, or those in power call good.

Terrorism, a war begun by our country from faulty and misused evidence, the abuse of prisoners, these and other recent events have shattered both lives and beliefs. To watch violence committed in the name of God and goodness can readily produce skepticism about God and cynicism about humanity. It is a despair that I have felt. Yet I remember feeling this same confusion and anguish when I saw the places in Britain and on the Continent where Catholics and Protestants, Anglicans and dissenters, were martyred, that is to say, murdered by one another, in the religious wars of the sixteenth and seventeenth centuries. The truth about being human seems to be that there is nothing that infallibly saves us from confusing evil with good, or worse with better, and that should not be surprising. Plato knew that a thing can be good in this way but not in that, here and not there, now and not then. He knew that there are many defective and even conflicting images of the Good. Yet none of this implies that we are not, most fundamentally, drawn to the good. And none of it shows that there is nothing to ground our choice.

In *The Ethics of Authenticity* Canadian philosopher Charles Taylor described the "authenticity" valued by modern Western cultures as the freedom each of us has to shape our lives according to our own sense of who we are and what we take to be of value. Yet Taylor also argued that authenticity need not mean, in fact, cannot mean, that there is no value apart from the decision that something is of value. If what is good were something created by our decisions, then choice would lose its significance, Taylor said. If we believe there is good only in the choosing, "at one moment we understand our situation as one of high tragedy, alone in a silent universe, without intrinsic meaning, condemned to create value." But then, "at a later moment, the same doctrine, by its own inherent bent, yields a flattened world, in which there aren't very meaningful choices..." To decide for oneself what is of value is to take responsibility for one's values; it cannot be to confer value.

To the question whether the good is created by us, individually or collectively, or whether it transcends us and is not created but found, it seems to me that Christianity has an interesting answer. We are to hold fast to what is good, and there is a good to hold fast to. We are called to love God and neighbor, and the good in that is neither arbitrarily self-chosen nor is it arbitrarily imposed. When we ask whether meaning is something we create from within our own lives, or whether it is something we find, incarnation suggests that it is both. And in the claim that the divine becomes human and the human divine, value can transcend us without being alien.

Turning inward to find God was conceived in ancient thought, pagan and Christian, with an understanding of the self that included much less of our distinctiveness than we insist upon now. For Plotinus the self turns out to be barely distinct from the One. Even Augustine, for all his narrative skill, seems to be telling the story of his life before conversion more as a way of exploring why it took him so long to discover the Beauty of God than because he saw his history as constitutive of who he was.

Nevertheless, the concept of incarnation fits at least as well, and arguably better, with thought that values individuality more. Perhaps Maximus the Confessor in the seventh century was one of the first Christian writers to recognize this. He saw the differences between and within species as intrinsic to created being and as good. In our own time, in *New Seeds of Contemplation*, Merton expressed the idea more lyrically: "My true personality will be fulfilled in the Mystical Christ in this one way above all, that through me, Christ and His Spirit will be able to love you and all men and God the Father in a way that would be possible in no one else." "Because God's love is in me," he continued, "it can come to you from a different and special direction that would be closed if He did not live in me, and because His love is in you, it can come to me from a quarter from which it would not otherwise come." For Merton, God is incarnate in us, and our uniqueness matters.

Traveling throughout France after leaving Grandchamp, I often thought about medieval peasants who would lay their hoes upon the ground and start the long trek to Mont St. Michel. To me their journey sounded romantic, and I knew it could not be mine. Those peasants would have known where they were going, and even if their path was perilous, they could anticipate their journey's end. I sometimes propose to a student troubled by the inconclusiveness of philosophy that one of the tasks of human life in our time is to learn to live gracefully in the midst of deep uncertainty. We differ from one another in our interpretations of experience and in our hypotheses. We differ in our willingness to speculate at all.

It seems likely to me that I live with deeper uncertainties than did my mother, even though, as in so many things, I cannot be sure. But watching her in the hospital so many years ago, what impressed me more than anything she could have said was the courtesy with which she greeted the nurses, however much she was in pain. I could wonder whether that is an actual memory, except that at my father's funeral I happened to meet one of my mother's nurses. After all those years and all the patients she must have had, that nurse remembered my mother, and she told me my mother was one of the loveliest people she had ever known.

So this is my sense of what ultimately matters. It is something I once heard Ann Ulanov say: "Never perjure the good." I did not ask Ann what she meant, and I often fail to live into what I think I know. But this is how I understood her words: never ignore the good or be dismissive of it, denying that it is good. Never be careless of it or reject it or refuse to respond to it with love. And never receive what is good without gratitude.

www.ingramcontent.com/pod-product-compliance
Lightning Source LLC
Chambersburg PA
CBHW022016300426
44117CB00005B/222